STRATEGIC STUDIES INSTITUTE

The Strategic Studies Institute (SSI) is part of the U.S. Army War College and is the strategic-level study agent for issues related to national security and military strategy with emphasis on geostrategic analysis.

The mission of SSI is to use independent analysis to conduct strategic studies that develop policy recommendations on:

- Strategy, planning, and policy for joint and combined employment of military forces;

- Regional strategic appraisals;

- The nature of land warfare;

- Matters affecting the Army's future;

- The concepts, philosophy, and theory of strategy; and,

- Other issues of importance to the leadership of the Army.

Studies produced by civilian and military analysts concern topics having strategic implications for the Army, the Department of Defense, and the larger national security community.

In addition to its studies, SSI publishes special reports on topics of special or immediate interest. These include edited proceedings of conferences and topically oriented roundtables, expanded trip reports, and quick-reaction responses to senior Army leaders.

The Institute provides a valuable analytical capability within the Army to address strategic and other issues in support of Army participation in national security policy formulation.

Strategic Studies Institute
and
U.S. Army War College Press

ARAB THREAT PERCEPTIONS AND THE
FUTURE OF THE U.S. MILITARY PRESENCE
IN THE MIDDLE EAST

W. Andrew Terrill

October 2015

*****

Comments pertaining to this report are invited and should be forwarded to: Director, Strategic Studies Institute and U.S. Army War College Press, U.S. Army War College, 47 Ashburn Drive, Carlisle, PA 17013-5010.

*****

*****

The Strategic Studies Institute and U.S. Army War College Press publishes a monthly email newsletter to update the national security community on the research of our analysts, recent and forthcoming publications, and upcoming conferences sponsored by the Institute. Each newsletter also provides a strategic commentary by one of our research analysts. If you are interested in receiving this newsletter, please subscribe on the SSI website at *www.StrategicStudiesInstitute.army.mil/newsletter*.

FOREWORD

The Middle East is currently in one of its most dramatic periods of turbulence since the post-World War I emergence of the modern state system in that region. Recently, the United States and its Arab allies have been concerned by a number of distressing regional trends including the uncertain future of Iranian influence throughout the region, the rise and persistence of the Islamic State (IS) organization, the ouster of Yemen's Abd Rabbuh Mansur Hadi government from the capital of Sana'a and that country's subsequent civil war, and the rise of insurgencies in Libya, Egypt, and especially the Sinai.

The intense unrest in the Middle East has created new conflicts, but it has also brought some of the regional status quo powers into a greater level of cooperation to help address these problems. Saudi Arabia has emerged as a significant regional leader, almost by default, as other important Arab states such as Iraq, Syria, Egypt, and Libya have been struggling with domestic crises. Since the ouster of Egypt's Muslim Brotherhood government in July 2013, Riyadh and Cairo have maintained what often appears to be an important and stable working relationship. Saudi Arabia and other Gulf countries have provided billions in aid to the Abdel Fattah el-Sisi government in Egypt, and Riyadh and Cairo have discussed dramatically increased military cooperation.

The Arab states aligned with the United States currently are facing a number of particularly serious regional policy problems and remains an incubator of radicalism and terrorism. The Syrian civil war currently presents few scenarios for a decent outcome and continues to consume massive numbers of lives.

Iraq is also deeply troubled, with large portions of its northern territories including the city of Mosul still controlled by the IS organization. Other problem areas include Yemen and Libya, where dramatic domestic upheaval is continuing. In Egypt, President Sisi's iron fist approach to a Sinai-based domestic insurgency has been unsuccessful in defeating the terrorists or containing the conflict, which is growing. Finally, the Iranian nuclear agreement between that country and a number of major powers led by the United States has generated considerable unease among some Arab countries fearful of an Iran no longer constrained by sanctions.

Under these circumstances, the serious and mutating problems facing both the United States and the conservative Arab states are likely to cause both friction and cooperation between allies. The Saudis and other Gulf Arab oil producers also fear that new sources of global energy and more efficient usage of that energy have made them less important to the United States. As these problems become more complex, Arab allies are also aware that for now they have few other options for great power support beyond the United States. Russia has provided support to the hated Assad regime in the Syrian civil war and has little influence in the region except with Syria and Iran. Beijing's clout in the region tends to be financial rather than military, and China does not currently have military forces in place to defend the Gulf Arab states from Iran even if it wanted to do so. While China is deeply interested in increasing its maritime capabilities, serious military power projection into the Gulf region seems a distant prospect.

The Strategic Studies Institute is pleased to offer this monograph as a contribution to the national security debate on this important subject as our nation continues to grapple with a variety of problems associated with the future of the Middle East. This analysis should be especially useful to U.S. strategic leaders, policy analysts, and intelligence professionals as they seek to address the complicated interplay of factors related to regional security issues, fighting terrorism, and the support of local allies. This work may also benefit those seeking a greater understanding of long range issues of Middle Eastern and global security. It is hoped that this work will be of benefit to officers of all services as well as other U.S. Government officials involved in military and security assistance planning.

DOUGLAS C. LOVELACE, JR.
Director
Strategic Studies Institute and
    U.S. Army War College Press

ABOUT THE AUTHOR

W. ANDREW TERRILL joined the Strategic Studies Institute (SSI) in October 2001, and is SSI's Middle East specialist. Prior to his appointment, he served as a Middle East nonproliferation analyst for the International Assessments Division of the Lawrence Livermore National Laboratory (LLNL). In 1998-99, Dr. Terrill also served as a Visiting Professor at the U.S. Air War College on assignment from LLNL. He is a former faculty member at Old Dominion University in Norfolk, Virginia, and has taught adjunct at a variety of other colleges and universities. He is a retired U.S. Army Reserve Lieutenant Colonel and Foreign Area Officer (Middle East). Dr. Terrill has published in numerous academic journals on topics including nuclear proliferation, the Iran-Iraq War, Operation DESERT STORM, Middle Eastern chemical weapons and ballistic missile proliferation, terrorism, and commando operations. He is also the author of *Global Security Watch – Jordan* (Praeger 2010). From 1994-2012, Dr. Terrill participated in the Middle East Regional Security Track 2 talks, which were then part of the Middle East Peace Process. He has also served as a member of the military and security working group of the Baker/Hamilton Iraq Study Group throughout its existence in 2006. Dr. Terrill holds a B.A. from California State Polytechnic University and an M.A. from the University of California, Riverside, both in political science. He also holds a Ph.D. in international relations from Claremont Graduate University, Claremont, California.

SUMMARY

The threat perceptions of many Arab states aligned with the United States have changed significantly as a result of such dramatic events as the 2011 U.S. military withdrawal from Iraq, the emergence and then fading of the Arab Spring, the rise of Iranian power and Tehran's nuclear agreement with key world powers, the Egyptian revolution and counterrevolution, and the development of civil wars in Syria, Iraq, Yemen, and Libya. A particularly worrisome development and expansion has been the dramatic rise of the "Islamic State" (IS) organization which has seized considerable tracts of territory in Iraq and Syria and inspired terrorists throughout the region. Elsewhere in the region, the 2013 election of the pragmatic and statesmanlike Iranian president Hassan Rouhani is viewed by some Arab states as a potential opportunity but also a danger since the new Iranian government has a potentially shrewder and more effective president and cabinet than seen during the Ahmadinejad years. There have also been some notable differences that have developed between the United States and its Arab allies over how to address these issues and most especially Iranian regional ambitions.

Some Arab leaders, including a number of Saudis and other Gulf Arabs, have subtly but publicly criticized the United States for appearing to lose interest in the Middle East as it becomes less dependent on that region's energy and due to serious problems encountered with the U.S. military intervention in Iraq. Many Arab states are also concerned that the United States may become increasingly interested in disengaging from the problems of the Arab World at a time when increased U.S. attention may be required to address the discord over the South China Sea and emerging problems in Eastern Europe and particularly Ukraine. To these Arab states, other regions are something of a distraction and they see any increased U.S. attention on Asia or Eastern Europe as a potential long-term national security problem. Moreover, while the rise of the Islamic State (IS) organization has refocused U.S. attention on the Middle East, most conservative Arab states remain concerned about retaining a sustained U.S. commitment to the region and are worried that Washington and Tehran are in considerable agreement over the danger posed by IS, even as they are distrustful of each other.

U.S. efforts to prepare for conflicts in the Middle East consequently remain vital, and doing so through actions which deter such conflicts is an especially optimal outcome. Shaping the Middle East strategic environment through carefully tailored collaboration with Arab partner nations presents one of the best ways to both prepare for a potential conflict and to deter that conflict through U.S. and allied defense preparedness. In this environment, it is important that Washington has an array of options that can be used to support and reassure local allies and deter aggression so that the threat of war can be averted before it is realized. The United States continues to project its interest in the region through a number of ways examined in this work including multilateral exercises such as Eager Lion in Jordan, regionally aligned forces, military forward presence, and military advice and assistance. Even with increased energy independence, the United States maintains a number of core interests in the Middle East and is often drawn back to the emerging problems and crises there. In parallel, the conservative Arab states are aware that they have no good

alternative to the United States as their most important security partner at the present time. A variety
of U.S. officials are committed to a strong effort to
convince Arab allies that the United States will not
abandon them or downgrade the importance of their
security concerns.

ARAB THREAT PERCEPTIONS AND THE FUTURE OF THE U.S. MILITARY PRESENCE IN THE MIDDLE EAST

Introduction: Protecting U.S. Interests in the Arab World in a Time of Global Change.

The Middle Eastern strategic environment has been especially dynamic in the last decade due to factors such as the 2003-11 U.S. combat operations in Iraq, the Arab Spring uprisings and attempted uprisings, the rise of Iranian power, the Egyptian revolution and counterrevolution, the Syrian civil war, the emergence of the Islamic State organization in Syria and Iraq, the danger of al-Qaeda affiliates in various countries including Syria and Yemen, and the continuing rise in sectarian tensions and violence throughout a number of regional countries, including some enveloped in civil war. All of these developments are of deep interest to Middle Eastern regional powers and to extra-regional powers that are involved in the Middle East including the United States. This monograph is focused on the conservative Arab states aligned with the United States, especially Egypt, Jordan, and the Gulf monarchies. It does not address Arab-Israeli relations which have been comprehensively discussed elsewhere.[1] Additionally, some major Arab states such as Egypt and especially Iraq are currently so focused on domestic turmoil that they can direct only limited attention to foreign policy issues that do not impact them in a direct, short term way. These states sporadically assert themselves on a variety of some key issues.

In the midst of changing Middle East developments, the stability of the Arab world remains of critical importance to the United States, despite strategic

1

challenges in other parts of the world. Numerous U.S. presidents have emphasized their country's commitment to Middle Eastern defense and enumerated the U.S. interests in the region that need to be protected.[2] In a recent example, President Barack Obama has stated that U.S. "core interests" in the Middle East include: (1) safeguarding energy supplies exported to the world, (2) counterterrorism, (3) countering the proliferation of nuclear weapons and other weapons of mass destruction, and (4) the defense of Israel and advancement of the Arab-Israeli peace process.[3] Other recent and contemporary U.S. political and military leaders have elaborated on the President's views by noting the Middle East will remain vital to Washington even as the United States moves closer to energy independence.[4]

Obama's comments indicate that U.S. interests in the Middle East have become more complex in the last few decades and can no longer be reduced to the traditional goals of access to energy products at reasonable prices and support for Israel, although these concerns remain important. In this regard, new oil and gas discoveries within the United States, new technologies for energy extraction, and progress with alternative energy sources have made the United States significantly less dependent on Middle Eastern energy over the last 5 years.[5] Nevertheless, U.S. energy interests extend beyond the country's own imports. Serious conflict in the region can disrupt global energy markets and therefore hurt the U.S. economy. Moreover, a number of U.S. allies in Western Europe and Asia are nowhere near energy independence and will need continuing access to Gulf energy resources for the foreseeable future.

More strategically, the United States garners significant global influence by using its diplomatic and military clout to guarantee freedom of navigation for the transportation of Persian/Arabian Gulf energy supplies.[6] All states importing or exporting energy products from the Gulf consequently maintain an interest in U.S. policy toward the region. If the United States relinquished this position, a strategic vacuum would be created. Other powers, such as China or eventually even a resurgent Russia, under some circumstances may become interested in expanding their roles in the region, although they will not be able to replace the United States in any reasonable short- or medium-term scenario.[7] In recent years, China has expanded its diplomatic and commercial presence in the Middle East and especially commercial relations with Saudi Arabia, although it currently maintains only a limited military presence in the Gulf.[8] Moreover, at this time, Beijing is basing most of its growing blue water navy in Asian waters. It is doubtful China would expend significant resources to seek a major role as a Gulf military power, while facing geopolitical concerns and territorial disputes in the Pacific Ocean region.[9] Chinese military ambitions in the Middle East would also alarm India which has increased its naval budget in response to previous expansions of Chinese naval activity.[10] Additionally, most Arab states would prefer to retain the United States as the guarantor of Gulf Arab security if this option remains open. These nations do not consider Russia or China to be their natural allies and are concerned about Russian and Chinese ties to Iran and Moscow's strong support for Syria's Bashar Hafez al-Assad regime.

In recent years, the U.S. leadership has put forward the strategy of a rebalancing of its military forces to meet needs in Asia, essentially to reassure U.S. and Asian allies that they will not be abandoned in the face of rising Chinese military power.[11] This strategy seems to have declined in urgency as new U.S. security concerns have escalated in countries such as Iraq and Syria. Nevertheless, the level of discord between China and some other Asian states has intensified over disagreements on issues such as island sovereignty and the establishment of the Chinese air defense identification zone (ADIZ) over the East China Sea on November 23, 2013. U.S. allies (such as Japan and the Philippines) and even neutrals (such as Vietnam) in Asia have sought to consolidate and improve their ties with Washington as they have become increasingly concerned about China. While the planned intensification of U.S. focus on Asia has been limited by serious problems in the Middle East including the rise of the Islamic State (IS) organization in Syria and Iraq, it could easily re-emerge in response to a deepening crisis there.

The legacy of U.S. participation in the Iraq War (2003-11) is an important factor in the internal U.S. debate on Middle Eastern military policy since that conflict has generated increased public and policymaker aversion to the use of military force (and especially ground forces) to fight major wars and then engage in long occupations, nation-building efforts, and counterinsurgencies. The United States lost almost 4,500 troops in the Iraq War, with a much larger number of wounded. The direct costs of the conflict were $804 billion from 2003 to 2011.[12] These negative consequences were not widely foreseen prior to the invasion, and the George W. Bush administration initially suggested the war would be quick, one-sided, and would not require a lengthy occupation with a large number of troops.[13] Unrealistic expectations of rapid and easy victory in Iraq in 2003 have sometimes made it much more difficult for contemporary policymakers to gain public support for even the limited use of force to address international concerns where there is a fear of expanding and deepening involvement in an ongoing conflict (often referred to as "mission creep").[14]

While still in office, former Secretary of Defense Robert Gates stated:

> In my opinion, any future defense secretary who advises the President to again send a big American land army into Asia or into the Middle East or Africa should have his head examined, as General MacArthur so delicately put it.[15]

Obama has never been this blunt, but he consistently indicates that he will seek to avoid using massive conventional military force except in cases involving a U.S. national survival interest. [16] In his 2014 State of the Union address, Obama stated:

> I will not send our troops into harm's way unless it is truly necessary, nor will I allow our sons and daughters to be mired in open-ended conflict. We must fight the battles that need to be fought, not those that terrorists prefer from us — large scale deployments that drain our strength and may ultimately feed extremism.[17]

These concerns are clearly reflected in the administration's efforts to address the IS threat without the use of U.S. ground units in direct combat so long as this is possible.

A planned summer 2013 limited attack on Syria with air strikes and cruise missiles to deter the Assad government from the future use of chemical weapons faced furious opposition from domestic critics and public opinion.[18] Likewise, Obama's decision to use air strikes against IS and deploy U.S. military advisors and technical specialists to Iraq over the course of 2014 faced some public doubt, although these actions were less controversial than the potential strike on Syria, and significant elements of the U.S. public were willing to support air strikes against IS radicals. Support for U.S. military action in Syria and Iraq escalated dramatically when IS began beheading U.S. and other hostages, with these events displayed on the Internet. In a surprising turnaround, significant elements of the public briefly expressed a willingness to use ground troops as part of the war against IS in the immediate aftermath of these events.[19]

The need for U.S.-led military intervention to stop IS expansion illustrates that understanding the dangers of future military interventions does not allow one to reach the conclusion that military actions and activities are no longer required to defend U.S. vital interests in the Middle East. In the future, other potential U.S. military actions in the Middle East may be widely recognized by the public as truly necessary. Some challenges to U.S. interests may not be viewed as immediate threats to national survival, but the long-term consequences of leaving these problems unaddressed are likely to involve factors relating to both U.S. global leadership and the U.S. economic future. If vital U.S. interests are strongly threatened in the future, large segments of the U.S. public may consider future military actions involving the defense of these interests to be "wars of necessity." Such interventions may still be required regardless of how conscientiously the U.S. leadership struggles to prevent such eventualities from playing themselves out.

The U.S. interests previously noted will need to be protected. Many Arab states (particularly in the Gulf) have important natural resources and a great deal of infrastructure wealth, and are correspondingly concerned about their limited capacity for self-defense. Gulf leaders also consider their countries vulnerable to military pressure or even attacks by larger neighbors as well as insurgencies along the lines of recent problems in Yemen and Iraq.[20] To deal with either type of contingency, friendly states will need limited but tangible allied support. Such strategies will need to be developed and refined to continue serving the interests already identified by Obama and his predecessors, in collaboration with regional allies. The United States will also have to make serious efforts to work through the problems with regional allies which have occurred in recent years and to find ways to reassure those allies about continuing U.S. interests in this vital region. In order to reduce the impact of these differences, Washington will need to understand regional threat perceptions regarding Iran, the Assad regime in Syria, IS, al-Qaeda affiliates, and other dangers.

Regional Threat Perceptions and the Syrian Civil War.

The Syrian civil war is an important national security concern for a variety of regional states. Saudi Arabia and Qatar were especially interested in shaping the outcome of the war and provided significant supplies of arms to non-IS, anti-Assad rebels. While the Saudis and many of their allies made the ouster of the Assad regime their initial priority for Syria, not all Arab nations felt this concern with the same degree of urgency. Iraq, under former Prime Minister Nouri al-Maliki's government, maintained a relatively pro-Assad foreign policy after 2011 to the extent it could do so without provoking a crisis with the United States.[21] The Lebanese government initially attempted to maintain its neutrality in the conflict as a strategy for avoiding being drawn decisively into the bloodshed, but it now seems to view the IS and the al-Qaeda affiliated al-Nusra Front as more serious threats to Lebanese security than Assad. Lebanese authorities have already dealt with some Syrian-related violence in their country and fear a process of future escalation leading to another round of Lebanese civil war.[22] Egypt, while aligned with Saudi Arabia on most issues, has a much softer position on Syria. The Egyptians are opposed to Assad remaining in power but also stress that Assad's non-Islamist government will have to be part of a negotiated solution.[23] This viewpoint reflects Cairo's intense distrust of the Islamist rebel groups and in some ways parallels concerns expressed by U.S. leaders. Kuwait also called for a political solution to the crisis and other Gulf Cooperation Council (GCC) states may become more openly supportive of this solution over time in the face of mounting problems with IS.[24]

Many conservative Arab leaders, and especially those from Sunni monarchical regimes, have always disliked Syria's Alawite-led revolutionary "republic" under the Assads. This animus has become magnified as the Syrian death toll in the war mounted, and as the Saudis increasingly came to believe that the struggle in Syria has become a proxy war between their country and Iran, which is a strong Assad ally. Saudi Arabia and other conservative Arab states have also been distressed by U.S. policy toward the Syrian civil war. Early in the conflict, Saudi leaders argued that the United States had not done enough to help the rebels fighting against the Assad regime, and they argued for more lethal aid to moderate rebels and perhaps a no fly zone to halt the bombing activities of the Syrian Air Force.[25] The United States has been hesitant to insert itself into a central role in the Syrian civil war, although it has provided moderate groups with limited amounts of lethal aid and much larger amounts of nonlethal aid. In recent years, Washington has been concerned that the moderate elements within the Syrian opposition (except for Kurdish fighters) are not very viable and may either collaborate or in some cases expand existing collaboration with more radical groups or simply have their weapons taken from them by these groups, as has occurred in the past.[26] U.S. policymakers were particularly disturbed when TOW (tube-launched, optically tracked, wire-guided) anti-tank weapons provided to moderate rebels in 2014 came into the possession of the al-Qaeda affiliated al-Nusra Front, after they had either co-opted or defeated the groups that had originally received these weapons.[27] This situation changed when IS activities in Syria, and especially Iraq, became more threatening to larger regional interests, and the United States assembled a coalition of states to oppose IS. The most immediate result of this effort was the initiation of a U.S.-led bombing campaign against IS forces in Iraq and then Syria, and an effort to support the rebuilding of the Iraqi army, which will be discussed later.

A number of conservative Arab states were also critical of the U.S. decision in the summer of 2013 to stand down from a planned air and cruise missile attack on Syrian regime targets as punishment for Syrian use of chemical weapons against unarmed civilians in a suburb of Damascus.[28] The Saudis were particularly angry that the United States cancelled the strike against Syria in favor of a Russian-sponsored diplomatic solution to the problem of Syrian chemical weapons use. The clash of goals in this instance occurred because Washington was primarily concerned about enforcing the taboo against chemical weapons use in war and was not looking for an excuse to alter the balance of military power in Syria. Secretary of State John Kerry underscored the limited nature of the plan when he stated:

> We will be able to hold Bashar al-Assad accountable without engaging in troops on the ground or any other prolonged kind of effort in a very limited, very targeted, short-term effort that degrades his capacity to deliver chemical weapons without assuming responsibility for Syria's civil war.

He then added that the strikes would be an "unbelievably small, limited kind of effort."[29] Additionally, it now appears that Israeli Strategic Affairs Minister Yuval Steinitz, under instructions from Prime Minister Benjamin Netanyahu, informed the United States that his country favored a solution that could eliminate Assad's chemical weapons, which were originally developed and designed to use against them.[30] These weapons would have remained a threat to Israel if the regime retained them, but might emerge as an even greater threat if they were seized by terrorists. Consequently, Israel favored the destruction of Syrian chemical weapons stocks rather than a punishment raid.

Another way that Saudi Arabia has expressed its unhappiness with the U.S. approach to the conflict is through its policies involving potential spillover from the Syrian civil war.[31] Riyadh has agreed to provide the Lebanese Army $3 billion to purchase weapons primarily from France and thereby strengthening the Lebanese capacity to maintain its internal security while possibly weakening the position of the pro-Iranian militia, Hezbollah.[32] The agreement also includes training programs for the Lebanese Army conducted by the French military.[33] Weapons deliveries, under this agreement, began in April 2015 and are expected to continue over the next 4 years.[34] The aid package favors the purchase of French weapons and equipment, a provision that may have been included to express Saudi dissatisfaction with Washington's policies on Iran and Syria.[35] Paris also maintained a clear hard line on Iranian nuclear weapons issues throughout the negotiations in Switzerland, which was reassuring to Riyadh.[36] Lebanon, for its part, has an extremely serious need for modern weapons to cope with spillover (including jihadist incitement and infiltration) from the Syrian civil war.

Over time, problems in Syria began to appear more far-reaching and complex. In the 2013-15 time frame, many Arab countries became increasingly concerned about IS actions and success throughout the Levant, while continuing to express their unwillingness to tolerate the continuation of the Assad regime.[37] Saudi Arabia and the United Arab Emirates (UAE) are also increasingly alarmed about domestic implications of this organization's success in Syria and Iraq and have dramatically strengthened their counterterrorism laws, especially the penalties for joining or supporting terrorist organizations such as the IS.[38] The UAE has even enacted a toleration law criminalizing insults against other religious sects and ethnicities or any act deemed to incite racial or religious hatred.[39] Saudi and Emirati anxiety about such issues can be placed into perspective when one considers the large numbers of foreign fighters entering Syria at this time. According to *The Washington Post*, up to 1,000 foreign fighters a month were entering Syria in late-2014, with about 16,000 already in place.[40] The national breakdown of this group is unclear, and it is not certain how many of them are joining IS, rather than other radical groups such as al-Nusra Front.

Following the summer 2014 disaster in Iraq, a variety of Sunni Arab countries were willing to join the international coalition organized by the United States to use airpower to fight IS in Syria and Iraq. Among the Arab states, Saudi Arabia, Jordan, UAE, and Bahrain sent aircraft to participate in the air campaign, while Qatar provided ground support for the Arab portion of the air campaign.[41] Units of these air forces conducted a limited number of bombing missions against both Iraqi and Syrian targets. Such actions were useful to the United States beyond their military value since the participation of these Sunni states in the coalition helps dispel any notion that Washington was unilaterally siding with Shi'ite-led regimes in Iraq and Syria against Sunni insurgents in a sectarian war. The Sunni Arab regimes are also almost certainly interested in participating in the coalition in order to have their views remain relevant for any future decisions regarding U.S. and regional policies for Iraq and Syria, especially in any final settlements of the conflicts.

Also in September 2014, the administration announced plans to help train and equip units of the Syrian moderate opposition, although this action was significantly less important than the bombing campaign. The program was expected to involve only around 5,000 Syrians at a time, who were to be trained and equipped for defensive warfare.[42] As of mid-2015, the U.S. portion of the training program for these troops had made almost no progress because of Syrian rebel desertions and a painfully slow vetting process for prospective participants.[43] Should such problems continue, it is doubtful that these fighters can become even a minor force in Syria where more powerful entities, including the Assad regime, al-Nusra Front, and especially IS, currently dominate the struggle for power. Despite such problems, various GCC states sometimes still assert that the anti-IS struggle cannot lead to a relaxation of pressure on Assad or a de facto alliance with his regime. These countries often maintain the tyranny of the Assad regime is directly responsible for the rise of radical groups including IS and al-Nusra. They maintain that defeating IS, while not addressing the reason it rose to prominence in the first place, is a self-defeating strategy.[44] This position sounds logical, but it also has problems since there are no good alternatives to these entities, and opposing both of them equally may not be realistic.

The United States, while continuing to stress that Assad has lost all legitimacy and must leave the country, calls for a negotiated political transition in Syria. The negotiated solution envisioned by U.S. leaders involves the current Syrian government (without Assad himself) but does not include IS or al-Nusra.[45] The Egyptian government, which detests Islamic radicals, is also interested in a political solution to the war that provides some major role for secular leaders while freezing out radical jihadists. Jordan, which was deeply anti-Assad in the first years of the civil war, now appears to have decided that IS is the bigger threat. This change has caused the Jordanians to disengage from some of the anti-Assad forces they previously supported and explore the possibility of working more intensively with tribal forces that are fighting IS rather than the Syrian government.[46]

As noted earlier, the Iranian role in the Syrian civil war is quite important and is a source of ongoing frustration to the conservative Arab states. Iran provides the Assad regime with financial support, military advisors, weapons, and diplomatic support. Iran's al-Quds Force (an elite force of the Islamic Revolutionary Guards Corps or IRGC) has been especially active in training pro-Assad Syrian militias and providing the regime with significant military advice and technical assistance. Tehran has also strongly encouraged the deployment of thousands of Hezbollah militiamen from Lebanon to provide auxiliary infantry to the Assad regime. Iran remains strongly committed to Assad and can be expected to continue supporting his regime despite the economic sanctions that Tehran is currently enduring. In Nouri al-Maliki's last years as Iraq's prime minister, his government also sided with Assad in the unfolding civil war, although it did so in a more low profile way. Iranian-supported Iraqi Shi'ite militiamen have also participated in the conflict on the government's side, although virtually all of these forces are believed to have returned to Iraq after June 2014 in response to the crisis created by IS seizure of much of northern Iraq.[47]

The Saudis believed that the intense Iranian involvement in the Syrian conflict required a strong response. In the early years of the conflict, then head of intelligence, Prince Bandar pushed a very aggressive attempt to topple Assad by arming and supplying Syrian rebels.[48] Critics maintain that this effort included directing funds and transferring weapons to the more effective rebel fighting units with insufficient regard for the danger of radical ideology. The Saudis have responded that they have not supported or funded militant jihadists "of any kind."[49] The sincerity of these remarks is difficult to gauge, but Saudi Arabia has experienced a serious outbreak of al-Qaeda-sponsored terrorism within its own borders in the 2003-06 time frame. Saudi leaders seem to understand that, in an interconnected age, terrorist ideas cannot be confined within the borders of any one state. The Saudis are particularly concerned about the potential radicalization of portions of their youth and have imposed severe penalties for any person joining a radical organization. Saudis who join IS or another radical organization will not be able to safely return to their home countries without the fear of lengthy imprisonment or even the death penalty.

Even with Iranian help, the Syrian regime appears to be losing ground to IS and other radical guerrilla groups, while moderate Syrian fighters appear to have been completely overshadowed by the radicals. Antijihadist Kurdish fighters have fought well but there are limits to their geographic reach. The Syrian regime will probably be able to maintain control of territory in the Alawite areas and Damascus and survive in some form. Conversely, it is increasingly doubtful that the regime will recapture territory lost to IS in the north in the foreseeable future, and over time Assad may look more like a regional warlord than a national leader. Two major offensives in early-2015 collapsed in an indication of the staying power of IS and other rebel groups.[50]

Problems of the Islamic State and Long-Term Warfare in Iraq.

Although the conservative Arab states had a number of reasons to fear Saddam Hussein in the early-1990s prior to Operation DESERT STORM, he was widely viewed as less dangerous by the early-2000s due to his 1991 defeat and post-war sanctions. In the aftermath of the 1958 revolution against Iraq's Hashemite king, many of the remaining Sunni Arab monarchies viewed the safest and least revolutionary form of Iraqi government to have been a Sunni strongman who was able to suppress revolutionary activity among Iraq's Shi'ites. The conservative Arab states were never ideologically committed to democracy, and some of them were deeply uneasy about the U.S. decision to invade Iraq in 2003 to install a democracy that they expected to empower the Shi'ite majority. The rise of a Shi'ite dominated government in Baghdad was correspondingly alarming to Sunni-led states such as Saudi Arabia and UAE. Jordan and pre-civil war Syria also faced a huge influx of Iraqi refugees.

Sunni Arab concerns escalated following the U.S. military withdrawal from Iraq in 2011, when the Maliki government dramatically increased its aggressive sectarian behavior.[51] The Gulf press and various human rights organizations also suggest that Iraqi forces make frequent use of torture and the death penalty against Sunnis.[52] Most significantly for Iraq's future, Maliki arrested a number of important figures within Iraq's Sunni political establishment following the U.S. withdrawal, thereby eliminating key leaders of the Sunni community while intimidating the others. Eventually, Maliki sidelined most of Iraq's important Sunni political leaders and consolidated a special relationship with Iran to the enduring contempt of most Sunni Arab countries.[53] The repression, corruption, and sectarian basis of the Maliki regime provided a perfect incubator for the revitalization of the insurgency. Maliki refused to accept responsibility for these problems and claimed that jihadist activity in Iraq was solely the result of spillover from the Syrian civil war. Later, in a reflection of the poisonous regional atmosphere, he blamed Saudi Arabia, Qatar, and the UAE for "supporting terrorism" in Iraq.[54] This charge appears mostly unfounded, although some weapons supplied to Syrian rebel groups could have changed hands and ended up in Iraq.

In Iraq, IS's initial effort to capture key urban centers was directed at the Sunni cities of Anbar Province.[55] IS (then known as Islamic State in Iraq and the Levant [ISIL] or ISIS) then electrified the world with its northern offensive, which gave the organization its greatest victory. All four Iraqi army divisions stationed in the north collapsed rapidly when faced with jihadist assaults, and IS seized Iraq's second largest city, Mosul.[56] The militants then claimed to be planning to seize Baghdad, although this threat was never credible. At the time, IS had only 3,000-5,000 fighters in Iraq (with about the same number of allied auxiliary forces), while Baghdad is a city of over 7 million people, the majority of whom are hostile Shi'ites with their own militias.[57] Moreover, the Shi'ite religious leadership, including Grand Ayatollah Ali al-Sistani, called for Shi'ite militias to defend Baghdad as well as the Shi'ite holy cities of Najaf and Karbala. In displays of the most vulgar kind of raw sectarianism, IS calls Karbala "the filth-ridden city" and Najaf "the city of polytheism."[58] IS has also asserted that, once it had seized these cities, it would destroy their Shi'ite religious sites, which are among the most important of such shrines anywhere. In contrast to the Iraqi army, many of the Shi'ite militia were willing to fight to the last man to protect their holy sites.

Following the June 2014 rout of Iraqi security forces, IS declared an Islamic caliphate in the area that it controlled, and Abu Bakr al-Baghdadi, the organization's leader since April 2010, was declared "caliph" and the "leader of Muslims everywhere."[59] To underscore this claim, the organization began using the name Islamic State for the first time, replacing the name ISIL/ISIS and reflecting the organization's enhanced ambitions beyond Syria and Iraq. This statement claimed that IS was now the only legitimate authority in the Muslim world and that its authority superseded and replaced the leadership of each Muslim country. It also seems natural for the leaders of a self-styled Islamic caliphate to be extremely interested in seizing control of Islam's holiest cities of Mecca, Medina, and Jerusalem. Since Saudi Arabia controls the two most important of these cities, it would seem a natural target. Even with all of these warning signs, most of the Gulf monarchies continued to view Iran as their deadliest enemy in the immediate aftermath of the seizure of Mosul.[60] During the 2015 battle to recapture Tikrit from IS, the Iranian role in assisting Iraqi government forces was particularly worrisome to many Arab leaders. The IRGC provided artillery and rocket support to the Iraqi forces and may have participated in the assault against strong points within the city although U.S. air support eventually was called upon to break the back of IS resistance.[61] Former Saudi Foreign Minister Saud al-Faisal stated that Iran had attempted to use its role in proving military aid to Iraq as a way of "taking over" that country.[62]

As noted, most Gulf Arabs leaders, and especially the Saudis, detested former Iraqi Prime Minister Nouri al-Maliki throughout much of his time in office. While most Sunni Arab states were delighted to see him removed from power, many have continued to view the Iraqi government with suspicion. Iraqi Prime

Minister Haider al-Abadi seems to have earned some respect from Sunni Arab leaders by his apparently genuine efforts to reach out to Iraqi Sunnis, but many other Iraqi government leaders still view Iraq's Sunnis as enemies.[63] Highly sectarian Shi'ite cabinet members and other hardline government leaders have demonstrated considerable resourcefulness in preventing Abadi from implementing key reforms by establishing themselves as major power brokers.[64] In one particularly alarming example, they have been highly effective at limiting Iraqi government military aid for anti-IS Sunni tribes that the United States would like to supply with weapons to defend themselves against IS forces.[65] Instead, they strongly favored Shi'ite militias. Also, Iranian military aid to the Shi'ite militias is not new, but quickly increased and became more overt since the June 2014 defeats. Abadi has denied undue Iranian influence over his country, claiming that relations with Tehran are "very balanced" with ties with other important regional countries.[66]

In this difficult and uncertain environment, some Sunni Arab states have made an effort to improve relations with Iraq's post-Maliki government, despite their ongoing concerns about Iranian influence and the excessive sectarianism of some Iraqi cabinet members. In this spirit, the Saudi leadership has announced that it will reopen its embassy in Baghdad and open a consulate in Erbil (the capital of the Kurdish Regional Government) as soon as security conditions permit.[67] The Saudis had previously appointed an ambassador in 2009 but based him in Jordan, claiming that Baghdad was too dangerous for a permanent diplomatic presence. Diplomats from various countries had previously been kidnapped or killed in Iraq for several years after the removal of the Saddam Hussein regime, although this has not occurred in recent years except in territory overrun by IS forces.

Many leaders throughout the region increasingly view the future of Iraq as volatile with considerable potential for developments there to harm their own security for years to come. Sisi has stated, "[IS has] a plan to take over Egypt" which they hoped to implement after seizing Iraq, Syria, and then Jordan and Saudi Arabia.[68] States neighboring both Syria and Iraq are deeply concerned that IS-controlled areas could become a center of terrorist training, operational planning, and propaganda against their regimes. Additionally, Jordan and Lebanon have been swamped by large numbers of refugees from Syria and to a lesser extent Iraq. Jordan became especially concerned that the fall of Palmyra in Syria, around 150 miles from the Jordanian border, would increase the number of refugees flowing into the kingdom and would also escalate the risk of jihadist infiltration.[69]

Even prior to the rise of IS, Saudi Arabia has faced serious problems with terrorism including a dramatic bombing and terrorism campaign conducted by al-Qaeda within the Saudi Arabian homeland from 2003 to 2006. Since that time, a number of terrorist organizations have attempted to work with radical Saudis to strike against the government. Many of these people have been arrested in periodic sweeps, including individuals accused of receiving training from radical forces abroad, coordination with foreign terrorists, accumulating explosives or large numbers of weapons, harboring wanted individuals, and other such activities.[70]

Currently, IS also appears to be operating an uncertain number of cells in the Gulf monarchies. Saudi Arabia arrested a suspected IS operative in Riyadh in

April 2015 as a suspect in the murder of two police-men. The suspect told police that he was an IS member and had received weapons, money, and instructions from his IS handlers.[71] In a more sweeping event at approximately the same time, Saudi officials arrested 93 people suspected of being IS members living and operating within Saudi Arabia. These arrests included at least 65 Saudi nationals as well as a number of for-eigners within the Kingdom. Additionally, one cell that was swept up in the operation was reported to be planning a suicide car bombing against the U.S. embassy in Riyadh.[72] More arrests would come later as important portions of the network progressively unraveled in the face of Saudi police work.

The problem also acquired a new dimension be-ginning in November 2014 when some extremely mili-tant Sunni Saudi Arabians attacked a Shi'ite village in the Eastern Province's village of al-Dalwah, killing at least 8 people. IS did not claim responsibility for the strike and there are no indications of operational co-ordination with the attackers, but many of them had been previously jailed for jihadist activities including fighting in Syria.[73] The Saudi authorities moved quick-ly to arrest the suspects in the murders, clearly hop-ing to prevent the development of a cycle of terrorism and response. More recently, the previously unknown "Najd Province of the Islamic State" claimed several major Gulf attacks, which were also designed to sow sectarian discord.[74] The most serious of these attacks against a target in Saudi Arabia occurred in late-May 2015, when a suicide bomber attacked a Shi'ite mosque in al-Qadeeh village that killed 21 people and wounded nearly 100 others.[75] The group openly acknowledged that it was attempting to provoke a sectarian confrontation to help facilitate the fall of the Saud family.[76]

In addition to Saudi Arabia, the Najd Province has also struck in Kuwait. In a particularly horrific episode, a suicide bomber arriving from Saudi Arabia walked into the historic Imam Sadiq Mosque and blew himself up, killing 27 Shi'ite worshipers and wounding a staggering 227.[77] While the terrorist was clearly provided with the bomb and other forms of support inside of Kuwait, his handlers apparently believed that his identity as a foreigner would help to protect the Najd Province network inside of Kuwait. This belief seems to have been a mistake as Kuwaiti security forces moved intensively and aggressively to identify IS militants in their country. The Kuwaitis arrested at least 29 suspects, including 11 expected to be charged with murder for their roles in the mosque attack. The Kuwaiti government is expected to seek the death penalty in the trials of these individuals.[78] Some suspects were also released after they were questioned, and the authorities were satisfied that they were not involved.

Many Arab states are deeply concerned about the implications of IS sectarian terrorism, hatred, and incitement to violence within their home countries, especially in countries with significant numbers of Shi'ites including Bahrain, Kuwait, and Saudi Arabia. These countries may be particularly vulnerable should IS be able to incite extremist Sunni citizens to attack Shi'ite neighbors and thereby fan the flames of sectarianism to a degree that will be difficult to extinguish. Suspicious and sometimes hostile attitudes toward Shi'ites have existed in these societies long before IS became a factor and have generally increased as a result of increased sectarianism throughout the Middle East following the rise of a Shi'ite-dominated government in Iraq, but it is also true that both IS and al-Qaeda seek to make the situation worse and that IS propaganda identifies Shi'ites as heretics who have little, if any, right to even live.[79]

The technical and marketing effectiveness of IS propaganda is another important capability unmatched by earlier terrorist groups targeting the Gulf monarchies. While Saudi counterterrorism capabilities have improved dramatically over the past decade, Riyadh may now be facing a much more effective enemy than al-Qaeda in the field of propaganda warfare. Moreover, by seizing large areas of territory in Syria and Iraq and declaring a caliphate, IS also appears more successful than other terrorist organizations and correspondingly can emphasize major achievements. In response to the radical message, the Saudi leadership continues to emphasize the theme of IS and al-Qaeda as brutal, renegade groups that have nothing to do with true Islam, regardless of what they say. Saudi Arabia's leading cleric, Grand Mufti Sheikh Abdul Aziz al-Sheikh, has stated that ISIS and al-Qaeda jihadists are "enemy number one" of Islam and that their calls for jihad were issued on "perverted" grounds.[80]

There is also the question of IS infiltration into countries bordering Iraq and Syria. This danger is especially troubling for Saudi Arabia, which has a long border with Iraq. So far, only a very limited number of terrorist infiltration efforts have occurred from Iraq, although at least one of these was especially bloody. In this instance, in early-2015 four heavily armed men from Iraq attacked a Saudi border patrol force with suicide vests and automatic weapons. While all of these attackers were killed, three Saudi soldiers also lost their lives.[81] The Saudi Interior Ministry later announced that the attackers belonged to a "deviant group," a phrase that usually indicates al-Qaeda but would also seem applicable to IS.[82] In this difficult environment, Saudi Arabia is currently building a 900 kilometer security fence along its border with Iraq to help manage the problem of infiltration.[83] Jordan and Kuwait also have borders with Iraq, but they are much shorter and easier to monitor. The Kuwaitis, in particular, have also spent decades improving their border defenses with Iraq to the point that a serious infiltration danger probably no longer exists.[84] Additionally, unlike Jordan and Kuwait, Saudi Arabia has a long border with Yemen that needs to be protected. This problem became especially clear on August 6, 2015, when an IS terrorist wearing a suicide vest walked into a mosque frequented by the security forces in the southwestern city of Abha, near the Yemeni border, and managed to kill 15 people after detonating his explosives.[85] The terrorist, who was Saudi, is widely suspected of having infiltrated from across the Yemeni border, although this possibility remains unproven.

U.S. Arab Relations and the Challenge of Iran.

A number of Arab allies including Egypt, Jordan, and especially the GCC states have viewed the potential rise of Iran to nuclear weapons state status as a major national security issue.[86] This scenario may be averted for at least 10 years by the Joint Comprehensive Plan of Action (JCPOA) agreement arrived at by the United Nations (UN) Permanent 5 plus 1 (P5+1) negotiators, but serious concerns remain. In particular, the agreement does not and was never meant to help resolve non-nuclear regional issues. Thus, many differences remain unresolved. As noted earlier, most Gulf Arab states have experienced long-standing problems in their political relations with Tehran which have been aggravated by the rise of the

Iranian strategic threat following Iraq's collapse into chaos and Tehran's intense involvement in Syria, Iraq, Yemen, and elsewhere.

The Arab world correspondingly has a mixed but generally unfavorable response to the announcement in July 2015 that the United States and its partners had worked out an agreement on Iranian nuclear weapons and sanctions relief. The Iraqi leadership viewed the agreement with a sense of relief since that country's two primary supporters now appear less hostile to each other.[87] Oman, which is the only GCC state that maintains good relations with Iran, also approves of the agreement.[88] The leadership of Abu Dhabi in the UAE was deeply concerned about the agreement, although the leadership of the emirate of Dubai (also within the UAE) sees strong economic potential in the lifting of Iranian sanctions. Unsurprisingly, within the Arab world, the country most upset with the agreement is clearly Saudi Arabia. The Saudis appear less concerned with the technical aspects of the agreement than the potential for the United States to improve its relations with Iran, and the prospect of an economically stronger Iran due to sanctions relief.[89] Most other Gulf States are generally concerned as well, although they have not chosen to confront the United States publicly over the issue.

Many of the problems between Iran and various Arab states have been building for some time. In his book, *Duty*, Gates recounts his 2007 visit to Saudi Arabia and his meeting there with King Abdullah. This came at a time when public hostility between Iran and Saudi Arabia was less obvious, and Tehran and Riyadh did not yet have their current virulent disagreements over issues such as the Syrian civil war, the Saudi-led military intervention in support of Bahrain's monarchy, and years later the bombing of Yemen. Nevertheless, according to Gates, "[Abdullah] wanted a full-scale military attack on Iranian military targets, not just nuclear sites."[90] As these discussions progressed, Gates did not react well to the king's assertiveness, and he characterized Abdullah's comments as treating the U.S. military as "mercenaries." He further described the meeting by stating:

> The longer he talked, the angrier I got, and I responded quite undiplomatically. I told him that absent an Iranian military attack on U.S. forces or our allies, if the president [Bush] launched another preventive war in the Middle East, he would likely be impeached; that we had our hands full in Iraq; and the president would use force only to protect vital American interests.[91]

Gates also told King Abdullah that showing restraint was a sign of strength and not a sign of weakness as the king maintained. Four years later, in another meeting, King Abdullah graciously thanked Gates for his candor, although he might have preferred a different reaction.[92]

The cold war between Iran and some of the Gulf Arab states deepened significantly following the March 2011 Saudi-led GCC military intervention into Bahrain to support their monarchy and the outbreak of the Syrian civil war, which began in the same month.[93] Prior to the GCC move into Bahrain, the Iranians publicly supported the demands of Bahrain's mostly Shi'ite demonstrators, who called for a greater public role in the governance of the Sunni-led monarchy. These demonstrators were inspired by early days of the Arab Spring in which the governments of several other Arab countries already had been overthrown. The Manama government feared ouster and requested military and police support from its GCC partners. Saudi Arabia and the UAE agreed to provide the majority of forces for this intervention and met the Bahraini request. Tehran subsequently was infuriated by these actions which propped up an anti-Iranian monarchy just as it was being challenged by large-scale protests with at least some pro-Iranian elements among the protestors. Although the GCC intervention forces never actually fought against the demonstrators, their presence was highly significant in signaling wider support for Bahrain's government. Their deployment to protect key infrastructure and installations may also have freed Bahraini forces from some more routine duties so that they could more forcefully (and harshly) move against the demonstrators. Additionally, the outbreak of the Syrian civil war in the same month as the intervention in Bahrain further intensified Gulf Arab-Iranian tensions. The Saudi decision to intervene in Yemen, which will be discussed later, further damaged Iranian-Saudi relations. In the July 2015 Jerusalem Day demonstrations in Tehran, the House of Saud was unexpectedly denounced by protestors, in addition to the usual targets of Israel and the United States.[94]

Adding to the deterioration of Arab-Iranian relations at this sensitive time, some older antagonisms were further inflamed when a series of senior Iranian officials visited the disputed islands of Abu Musa and the Tunbs in 2012 and 2013 as a way of underscoring their physical control over them.[95] Then President Mahmoud Ahmadinejad visited the islands in April 2013 very late into his presidency.[96] The islands, originally seized by Iran in 1971, are also claimed by the UAE. UAE claims are strongly backed by the Arab League.[97] Tensions over these very small islands re-

main a central factor in complicating Iranian-UAE relations for mostly symbolic and national pride-related
reasons, although they have some strategic signifi-
cance as well due to their proximity to the Straits of
Hormuz. Ahmadinejad seemed to enjoy antagonizing
the Gulf Arabs for no clear foreign policy reason and
in sharp contrast to the measured approach of his suc-
cessor. Unsurprisingly, the depth of fear and distrust
in the UAE for the Islamic regime in Tehran is sometimes no less than in Riyadh, although as a smaller
country, it is more cautious about openly confronting
Iran.[98]

In contrast to their fears about an eventual Iranian
nuclear weapons capability, most Arab nations are
not deeply concerned about Iran's conventional forces, which are large but also have significant shortcomings. In this regard, a great deal of Iranian conventional military equipment is older and has been severely
worn by overuse. While the Iranian military should
be able to function effectively as a defensive force,
these units would have serious problems projecting
offensive power by crossing large tracks of hostile ter-
rain.[99] Tehran's ability to project conventional military
power across the Gulf is also limited by Iran's need
to circumvent or neutralize U.S., British, French, and
Gulf Arab naval forces stationed there. Iran's ability to
provide effective logistical support to its forces in hostile territory is especially doubtful, even with countries which can be reached without crossing the Gulf
(such as Iraq or Kuwait through Iraq).

The conditions of Iranian forces will almost certainly improve if the UN conventional arms embargo
is lifted in 2020 as envisioned in the JCPOA generated
by the Iranian nuclear negotiations, but even then
considerable money, time, and effort will be needed

to modernize Iranian forces. Iran has not had access to significant supplies of Western weapons since the fall of the Shah in 1979, and Iran has been under an effective UN arms embargo since 2010. This embargo effectively has blocked Iran from receiving conventional weapons from its most important post-1979 suppliers, including Russia and China.[100] Consequently, Tehran has been forced to rely extensively on its domestic arms industry, which is incapable of fully compensating for Tehran's inability to import modern weapons. The Russians have already indicated a strong desire to go forward with such sales and will probably push for the early lifting of the embargo to the extent that they can make any progress on this issue.[101] When the embargo is lifted, Iran can be expected to purchase systems such as the S-300 air defense missiles fairly rapidly, but it is unclear how quickly they will attempt to modernize their ground and air forces.

A more serious concern for many of the Arab states involves Iran's unconventional forces. Although Tehran's conventional military forces have major shortcomings, Iran has a strong capacity for waging asymmetric warfare with its naval and elite ground forces. Facets of this approach include the use of irregular forces and proxy forces, as well as covert arms transfers and providing training to such groups within a target country. One of Iran's most useful tools in projecting this kind of power is the IRGC's al-Quds Force. The al-Quds Force has a long record of working with pro-Iranian revolutionary groups in a variety of countries including Iraq and Afghanistan.[102] In both of these instances, they are also known to have supplied highly effective improvised explosive devices to anti-American forces.[103] In Syria, the al-Quds Force maintains an important role in supporting the Assad regime. While the al-Quds Force is not known to be playing a direct combat role in the war, its trainers and advisors have been invaluable in helping the government remain in power. The al-Quds Force willingness to help Assad is also underscored by the loss of five al-Quds Force generals in Syria in separate incidents since the beginning of the civil war. One of these generals was targeted and assassinated, while the others may have simply gotten too close to the fighting.[104] In Iraq, the al-Quds Force has played at least an equally important role as in Syria, training and supporting pro-government Shi'ite militias.[105]

Egypt, Saudi Arabia, the UAE, and some other Arab states are uneasy about the possibility that Tehran might be able to normalize its relations with the West at a time when many Arab-Iranian problems are unresolved. These states are also concerned that the United States may become increasingly interested in a "grand bargain" on IS and other regional issues with Iran as a way of de-escalating tensions with Iran at a time when increased U.S. attention is required in the South China Sea and Eastern Europe (especially the Ukraine) and when both Washington and Tehran are struggling against IS in Iraq.[106] In the past, many Arab states have been especially concerned about a U.S.-Iranian understanding, which resolves most of U.S.-Iranian differences and potentially leads the United States to take a much more sympathetic view of Iranian foreign policy.[107] Some Arab allies are also concerned that the United States might give too much away in a deal with Iran or begin to view Iran as a potential partner on some issues in Iraq and elsewhere. These states may also be unhappy over the United Kingdom's (UK) decision to re-establish diplomatic relations with Iran at the *charge d'affaires* level.[108] The

UK is Washington's closest ally, and its actions could easily be viewed as paving the way for a similar U.S. action.

A number of Arab leaders are also uncertain about the international implications of the leadership of Hassan Rowhani, the pragmatic Iranian president elected in 2013. Iran's former President Ahmadinejad could always be counted upon to make extreme statements that would infuriate and mortify the West, ensuring that little to no progress could occur in improving Iranian relations with the United States and Europe. Rowhani is nothing like his undiplomatic predecessor and openly called for reconciliation with the Gulf Arabs upon taking office. Later, after the announcement of the opening of nuclear negotiations with the P5+1, Foreign Minister Mohammad Javad Zarif visited a number of Gulf States including Kuwait, Oman, the UAE, and Qatar but not Saudi Arabia or Bahrain.[109] He travelled to these states to indicate an interest in better relations and assure these countries that the nuclear deal with the P5+1 would not be at their expense. Zarif has also indicated an interest in resolving the islands dispute with the UAE in sharp contrast to the rhetoric and symbolism of the previous government.[110] He expressed interest in visiting Saudi Arabia to discuss sustentative matters "when they're ready" and made a short mostly symbolic visit to Riyadh to pay Iranian respects after the death of King Abdullah in January 2015.[111] Unfortunately for Iranian moderates, Rowhani's restraint is not always matched by that of Iran's Supreme Leader Ayatollah Ali Khamenei, who often favors extremely harsh rhetoric.

While the prospect of any kind of breakthrough in U.S.-Iranian relations beyond the 2015 JCPOA is always worrisome to conservative Arab states, such an occurrence at this time may be particularly alarming with the GCC-Iranian cold war further escalating over Yemen (discussed later). If U.S. attention is more focused on Asia and Eastern Europe, there is concern that the United States may not wish to confront Iran. Some Arab leaders are worried that the United States has negotiated a less than optimal nuclear agreement with Iran.[112] Washington has also made an effort to insulate the nuclear talks from other issues, clearly indicating a belief that expanding the number of issues will over-complicate the talks and dramatically reduce already limited chances for success. This approach has not been agreeable to all U.S. allies. Saudi Arabia and Israel consistently have argued that any final deal over Iranian nuclear issues should also address regional issues, including Iran's role in Syria.[113] Conversely, Iranian Deputy Foreign Minister Abbas Araghchi told an Iranian State Television interviewer that a nuclear deal would not mean a normalization of ties with the United States.[114] This sentiment was echoed in a more authoritative way by Supreme Leader Ayatollah Khamenei after the conclusion of the JCPOA.[115]

Some Arab states are also uneasy that both the United States and Iran have made efforts to prop up the Baghdad government and worry that this common goal could lead to a wider relationship. They point to the fact that Washington has at least temporarily limited its criticism of significant, overt Iranian involvement in Iraqi defense and suggested that under some circumstances this involvement may yield positive results.[116] When asked about the possibility of increased cooperation with Washington on security matters as a result of the crisis, President Hassan Rowhani stated, "If we see that the United States takes action against terrorist groups in Iraq, then one can think about it."[117] The Gulf Arabs are often uneasy about any discussion of an expanded U.S.-Iranian relationship. Kerry has responded to this unease by noting that, at this point, the United States and Iran have a mutual interest but not a cooperative effort in Iraq. Obama has stated that he does not expect a "formal set of agreements" on U.S. and Iranian activities in Iraq but said U.S. officials would do their best to "de-conflict efforts by the U.S. and Iranian forces in that country."[118]

Saudi Arabia's leaders have also indicated that, if Iran ever acquires and deploys a nuclear weapon, they might be compelled to try to do the same thing and at this time, at least, reach the same level of nuclear infrastructure capability as Iran is granted under the JCPOA.[119] Such statements may be genuine, or they may be mostly bluster and anger. In the early-1970s, many within the Arab world clearly believed reports that Israel had acquired nuclear weapons, but they did not seek to match that capability. For Saudi Arabia to seek to acquire nuclear weapons in contemporary times would involve a series of political difficulties with the United States, Europe, other Arab states, and Israel. Building its own nuclear infrastructure encompassing the full nuclear fuel cycle and weapons cycle would be a difficult and lengthy project for a nonindustrialized nation such as Saudi Arabia.[120] Suggestions that Saudi Arabia might purchase nuclear weapons from Pakistan also seem far-fetched, since Pakistan would reap a variety of international repercussions from such actions. Additionally, the Pakistanis do not seem to have much difficulty refusing Saudi Arabian requests, including Riyadh's call for their participation in the air war against Houthi rebels in Yemen.[121]

Interestingly, on the basis of limited information, it also appears that Saudi citizens (like their leadership) consider Iran to be their more dangerous enemy. According to a public opinion poll conducted by the University of Wisconsin-Milwaukee and the Interdisciplinary Center of Herzilya, Israel, 53 percent of Saudis identified Iran as their country's main adversary, 22 percent said the Islamic State, and 18 percent said Israel. Even more unexpectedly, a quarter of the respondents maintained that Saudi Arabia should work together with Israel against Iran. The questioners told respondents that they were conducting the survey for the International Data Corporation, but did not further identify the center or associate it with Israel.[122] While the Saudi government is seldom led by public opinion, they also seem to be becoming more open to Israeli contacts. At a 2015 conference in Washington, Saudi Arabian and Israeli participants admitted that representatives of their countries had held a series of meetings on regional security issues.[123] It is possible these ties will grow in response to the strenuous objections both countries have about the July 2015 P5+1 agreement with Iran. Jordan and Egypt, which have diplomatic relations with Israel, may also be expanding their relations with the Israelis.[124]

The Role of Egypt and Libya in Middle Eastern Security.

The United States and many Arab states experienced some friction over policy differences involving Egypt as far back as the ouster of Egyptian President Hosni Mubarak in 2011. As the Mubarak government teetered, U.S. leadership had a choice of either maintaining its support for the Egyptian president or switching its backing to the demonstrators challenging him. This was not an easy decision and required a careful balancing of national objectives and values. Mubarak had been a longtime ally and a strong supporter of the 1979 Egyptian peace treaty with Israel and the struggle against Islamist terrorist groups such as al-Qaeda. Conversely, the demonstrators were clearly calling for democracy and expected U.S. support for their efforts to overthrow a friendly, but nevertheless highly autocratic regime. U.S. leadership avoided strongly committing to either side in the early stages of the conflict and did not start to tilt toward the demonstrators until after a major Mubarak speech on February 1, 2011, where he offered few meaningful concessions.[125] U.S. policy toward the confrontation correspondingly satisfied virtually no one in the region. Young activists challenging the regime later expressed disappointment and strongly asserted that the United States waited until the Mubarak regime appeared doomed before switching its allegiance (a critique which probably went too far).[126] In contrast, Arab conservatives, and especially the Gulf monarchies, were quick to charge that U.S. leaders abandoned Mubarak despite his many years as an ally.[127] Gulf Arab leaders observing this process may have been particularly concerned that the United States would abandon them at some point for ideological reasons if their monarchical governments were ever challenged by a strong opposition demanding democracy or democratic reform.

Unexpectedly, the Mubarak regime (which had been in power for almost 30 years) proved remarkably fragile in the face of determined demonstrations and calls for its removal. Egypt's army, which had a long history of involvement in domestic politics, initially attempted to present itself as neutral and waited to see if Mubarak could de-escalate the crisis with promises of future concessions. Beginning on February 3, 2011, the military began to move toward an accommodation with the demonstrators as Mubarak proved increasingly incapable of pacifying or dispersing the crowd. On February 10, the Supreme Council of the Armed Forces (SCAF) issued a communique endorsing the "people's legitimate demands," effectively removing Mubarak from office.[128] The next day the military assumed a caretaker governance of the country.

The Egyptian military assumed authority in the immediate aftermath of Mubarak's ouster, but its most senior leaders and especially the elderly Defense Minister, Field Marshal Mohammad Tantawi, did not seem interested in ruling the country for a prolonged period of time so long as they were able to maintain the military's privileged place in society. The Muslim Brotherhood then rapidly emerged as a leading political player, although it suffered an especially serious setback when the Egyptian Supreme Court dissolved a friendly parliament on June 14, 2012. The Brotherhood then strongly rebounded when its candidate Mohammad Morsi won a mid-June run-off election with 51.7 percent of the vote.[129] This outcome is less impressive than it might initially seem, since Morsi was only able to gain approximately half the votes in an election against retired Air Force General Ahmad Shafiq, an important figure in the Mubarak regime.[130] In this election, only a little over half of eligible Egyptian voters participated, while the rest did not vote. Adding to Brotherhood concerns, the SCAF issued a decree severely limiting the powers of the presidency shortly before the election results were announced.[131] The SCAF based this proclamation on its status as the interim governing authority following Mubarak's ouster. Morsi took office as Egypt's president on June 30, 2012.

The Morsi Administration lasted for just over a year in power. This time frame was characterized by considerable political infighting and no clear progress in addressing Egypt's towering economic problems. On July 3, 2013, following several days of massive popular demonstrations against the government, the Egyptian military unilaterally dissolved Morsi's government and placed him under arrest for a wide variety of crimes.[132] Defense Minister General Sisi (who had replaced Tantawi) emerged as the most important figure in the ouster, although military leaders installed the Chief Justice of the Supreme Constitution Court as a figurehead president, pending new elections. In March 2014, Sisi resigned from the military to run for president. After winning the election, he assumed office in June. Morsi, by contrast, was sentenced to 20 years in prison in April 2015 after being convicted of inciting violence and directing illegal detentions and torture.[133] In May 2015, he was further sentenced to death, although it remains uncertain if this decision will ever be carried out.[134]

The United States was again caught in a difficult situation by the military's 2013 seizure of power from the incompetent although democratically elected Morsi government. Washington sought to continue good relations with Cairo, and the administration refused to label the ouster a coup. If U.S. leaders had done so officially, they would have been legally required to halt aid to Egypt, which they wanted to avoid.[135] Yet, while seeking to work with the Egyptians, Washington was also disturbed by substantial anti-democratic repression and ongoing excesses of the new government.

The Egyptian government designated the Muslim Brotherhood to be a terrorist organization following a suicide car bombing of a police headquarters that killed 15 people. The government never provided any evidence of the Brotherhood's involvement in the attack, although Sisi is openly determined to eradicate the Muslim Brotherhood.[136] He has also been prepared to accept a great deal of criticism over Egyptian human rights policies to do so.[137]

The actions of the Egyptian military in ousting Morsi were applauded by a number of conservative Arab states. As Sisi moved against the Brotherhood, he was strongly backed with financial support from Saudi Arabia and the UAE.[138] These wealthy countries sought to protect Sisi from potential U.S. pressure and provided the Egyptian leadership with political support for whatever harsh measures the Egyptian leadership considered necessary. In the aftermath of the military seizing power, there was considerable street unrest and bloodshed. Thousands of supporters of the Muslim Brotherhood and others were killed in street fighting with the police and army, often when government forces attempted to enforce a highly restrictive law regulating demonstrations. Huge numbers of both Islamist and secular dissidents were also arrested. The administration of justice appeared deeply flawed with some closed military trials for civilians and occasional mass sentencing on the basis of "trials" that lasted less than an hour and did not always allow defense attorneys to speak.[139] By April 2015, around 2,500 people had been killed in street violence, and more than 40,000 were incarcerated for anti-regime or pro-Islamist activities.[140] In line with the example of some other Arab states (such as the UAE), the Egyptian government has also moved to consolidate official control of the mosques by replacing pro-Brotherhood clergy with licensed state approved clerics, who can be trusted to give sermons adhering to strict government guidelines.[141]

In July 2013, the United States downgraded its military relations with Egypt as the result of the Egyptian military seizing power and the ongoing crackdown on dissents that followed this action. Prior to this disruption, the United States had provided $1.3 billion in aid to Egypt, the balance of which was military aid. This aid was scaled down in 2013 when delivery of high profile items including F-16 aircraft, M-1 tanks, and AH-64D Apache helicopters was suspended. These measures were adopted reluctantly due to Egypt's high value as a regional partner, and they began to be scaled back after less than a year. Correspondingly, on April 22, 2014, the United States announced that it would resume delivery of Apache helicopters to Egypt, citing that country's continuing commitment to the peace treaty with Israel.[142] The United States further released $650 million in other military aid to Egypt at the same time. These helicopters can be exceptionally helpful in the counterinsurgency operations, and there was a corresponding U.S. interest in transferring these items. Later, in April 2015, the United States lifted all remaining sanctions against the Egyptian military and restored the full military aid relationship. As a result of this change, the White House noted that the United States would be sending additional fighter jets, missiles and tank kits to Egypt, and that it would continue to provide $1.3 billion in military assistance for Egypt.[143] The U.S. leadership also has indicated that it hopes to shift Egyptian military aid away from tanks and fighter aircraft toward weapons and equipment designed to enhance counterterrorism capabilities and border and maritime security.[144] Egypt, however, has used air strikes against IS-affiliated forces in both Libya and the Sinai, and Egyptian leadership does not always seem to view counterinsurgency and conventional warfare in fundamentally different ways.

A major reason for the U.S. shift in military assistance policy involves the expansion of a serious Islamist insurgency centered in the Sinai Peninsula since Morsi's ouster. There have been a number of lawless elements in the Sinai for decades, but the collapse of the Mubarak government led to the withdrawal of a number of policemen from the area and opportunities for various groups to expand into a more formidable threat.[145] Currently, the militants are a mix of hardcore Egyptian Islamic extremists, radical Palestinians from nearby Gaza, foreign fighters, and disgruntled young Egyptian men who are angry about their poverty and lack of opportunities, according to Sinai residents.[146] Some convicts who escaped from prison during the uprising against Mubarak also joined the militants in Sinai.

The al-Qaeda group formerly known as *Ansar Beit al Maqdis* is the best known of the Sinai insurgent groups. In November 2014, the militants of this group abandoned their relationship with al-Qaeda and pledged loyalty to the IS caliphate, changing their name to the "Sinai Province of the Islamic State." This group apparently pledged loyalty to the IS in the hope that the group could give them money, weapons, tactical advice, and propaganda support that might help in recruiting.[147] It is not certain how much of this kind of support they received, although the group has increased their holdings of sophisticated weapons through smuggling enabled by the disarray of the Libyan civil war and the availability of weapons once under the control of the Libyan military.[148] In this environment, hundreds of Egyptian soldiers and policemen have died since July 3, 2013, many in attacks by Muslim militants in Sinai but also in acts of terrorism throughout Egypt.

While Morsi was in power, he is believed to have sought negotiations with some of the less radical Sinai groups and also hoped to develop the peninsula economically in order to reduce the causes of instability, radicalism, and violence.[149] However enlightened this approach may have seemed, it was too one-dimensional to succeed and, as noted, allowed these groups to grow. The Sisi government has responded to this threat in a radically different but equally one-dimensional manner, with an emphasis on military means. Thus far, such iron fist policies have not defeated the Sinai Province organization and other terrorist groups, nor have they reduced their ability to engage in complex terrorist strikes. In one particularly deadly attack on October 24, 2014, at least 33 soldiers were killed.[150] The government responded to this disaster with a rapid decision to demolish houses on the Egyptian side of the border with the Gaza Strip (with compensation to the owners) in order to create a buffer zone there. The government expects this buffer zone to help stem the flow of weapons and militants across the border.[151] Nevertheless, at the time of this writing, government forces, especially those in Sinai, continue to endure sophisticated attacks by terrorist forces. Police officers, soldiers, and security officials have been attacked at checkpoints, police stations, military camps, and while traveling in their vehicles. On July 1, 2015, in one particularly horrific effort, a wave of simultaneous attacks through Sinai killed 64 soldiers.[152] These ongoing security problems seem to indicate that Sisi's approach to internal security is not showing much success.

While Egypt has faced a number of challenges since Morsi's removal from power, it has continued to consolidate its relations with a number of important regional allies. Saudi Arabia and Egypt have a number of overlapping security interests and have coordinated on all major regional security issues, although the policy views of each county's leadership are by no means identical on some important issues such as the war in Syria. The Gulf Arab states (except for Qatar) were openly hostile to the U.S. decision to hold the Egyptian Army even minimally responsible for the 2013 ouster of a democratic government and its violent aftermath. Many of these states were worried about the possibility of an Egyptian rapprochement with Iran under Morsi, which seemed possible despite the strong differences between Tehran and Cairo on the Syrian revolution. The process reached a point of alarm following then-President Ahmadinejad's visit to Cairo in early-2013.[153] Israel is also supportive of the Sisi government and strongly favors efforts by the United States to continue providing Cairo with weapons. Like the Egyptians, Israelis are deeply concerned about the insurgency in the Sinai, which they view as a threat.

In addition to the terrorists operating out of Sinai, IS-affiliated forces in Libya have also struck at Egypt from Libya. In one particularly egregious episode, IS-affiliated terrorists kidnapped and then executed 31 Coptic Christian Egyptians who had been abducted from the city of Surt.[154] The Egyptian military responded with a February 16 air strike on what were described as IS camps, training centers, and weapons storage areas in Libya.[155] These attacks did not deter IS from engaging in other atrocities, and in April 2015, IS released a video showing the execution of dozens of

42

Ethiopian Christians by shooting and beheading.[156] IS-affiliated fighters in Libya have also claimed responsibility for attacks on Libyan government buildings, foreign embassies, a major Libyan oil field, and militias based in the city of Misurata.

IS forces did not appear in Libya until 2014, but they have expanded dramatically since that time and may currently have as many as 3,000 fighters.[157] IS in Libya has been able to survive because of the security vacuum that has resulted from two rival political leaderships, each claiming to be the legitimate government. The internationally recognized government, which is led effectively by General Khalifa Haftar, is based in the eastern cities of Tobruk and Bayda, while the pro-Islamist Libyan Dawn government is based in Tripoli. Hiftar is a Qadhafi-era general who defected in 1990 and returned to Libya following the outbreak of civil war in 2011. Haftar's government is strongly supported by Egypt's President Sisi and by other conservative Arab governments, which have been shocked by the rapid development of the Libyan IS threat.[158]

The rival governments have often seemed more intent on fighting each other than on fighting IS.[159] This situation may improve as a result of UN-sponsored unity talks, but this remains uncertain. IS currently controls the large coastal city of Surt and until late-July 2015 maintained militia in the eastern city of Derna. The force in Derna has now been driven out of the city by local Islamists, who did not wish to cede their authority to IS.[160] This is an interesting example since some other local militias may also be willing to resist any IS incursions into areas under their control, and thus limit IS opportunities, even in the absence of a unified Libyan government. Unfortunately, it is not clear that this factor will be decisive in all future instances. The Libyan branch of IS has also been reported to be extremely close to the main organization with its headquarters in Syria, so it may be able to obtain meaningful assistance with recruiting and funds from this source.[161]

The Ongoing Crucible of Yemen.

Yemen is a large, important, but also economically impoverished Arab country having a lengthy border with Saudi Arabia and direct access to key strategic waterways including the Red Sea and the Gulf of Aden. It is currently the only nonmonarchy on the Arabian Peninsula as well as one of that region's more heavily populated countries, with around 24-25 million people. Yemen's most important political figure from 1978-2012 was then-President Ali Abdullah Saleh, who left office in February 2012, during the Arab Spring, as the result of massive and unrelenting domestic, regional, and international pressure for him to resign. In this chaotic environment, Yemen's Gulf neighbors became concerned about the escalating crisis in that country and the prospects for spreading instability. The nations of the GCC states led by Saudi Arabia consequently played a major role in easing Saleh out of office. Saleh's Vice President Abd Rabbuh Mansur Hadi then became acting head of state and was elected president under a transition plan in which he was the only candidate on the ballot.[162]

Hadi never had the same kind of carefully cultivated power base as his predecessor and also lacks many of the former president's political skills. To the extent that he could, Hadi waged an uncompromising war against al-Qaeda in the Arabian Peninsula (AQAP), the most powerful and dangerous of the al-Qaeda affiliates. This effort produced important results but also required extensive funding from the GCC states and the U.S. support of the Yemeni armed forces with military training programs and the use of armed drones against terrorist targets.[163] Hadi was particularly assertive in a 2012 offensive against AQAP, which had previously seized a significant amount of territory in southern Yemen during the turmoil of the Arab Spring when Saleh was challenged and overthrown.[164] While Yemeni forces pushed AQAP out of the cities and towns that it had held prior to the offensive, the organization remained powerful and was still able to conduct spectacular acts of terrorism against government institutions.[165] During this military offensive, there were also some signs of problems within the Yemeni regular military, which often seemed to play a secondary role in the fighting. These soldiers were overshadowed by the extensive use of U.S. drones to disrupt AQAP command and control and perhaps more tellingly by the use of Yemeni tribal fighters for ground combat. These irregular tribal fighters were paid well with GCC money and have sometimes been referred to as mercenaries.[166] The need for tribal fighters as an indispensable element of the offensive was an important indicator of ongoing dysfunction within the regular military.

AQAP is usually perceived by Western analysts and policymakers as the dominant threat to Yemeni peace and security, but their activities have been greatly overshadowed by the Houthi movement, which seized the capital of Sana'a in September 2014. The Houthis are Zaydi Shi'ites who have maintained a long history of disagreement with the central government in Sana'a. Throughout the 1990s and 2000s, the Yemeni government aggravated its problems with the Houthis by allowing a number of Saudi funded missionaries to establish religious institutions in northern Yemen.[167] These institutions were designed to advance Sunni Salafi versions of Islam and seek converts among the Houthi citizens and youth. Such missionaries usually viewed Shi'ite religious beliefs in an unsympathetic and sometimes an outright toxic light, and their actions were viewed as confrontational and provocative by the Houthi leadership. The Yemeni government nevertheless did not wish to restrict the movement of these clerics into Yemen and thereby potentially offend Saudi Arabia, which was a chief source of Sana'a's foreign aid. The Yemeni government later attempted to arrest the Houthi leadership, sparking a series of counterinsurgency wars from 2004 until 2010.[168]

Saudi Arabia entered the anti-Houthi fighting for the first time in northern Yemen in November 2009. At this time, a group of Houthi rebels crossed into Saudi territory, killing at least two border guards and apparently taking control of two or more Saudi border villages. In response, Riyadh took swift and decisive action with military strikes against Houthi rebels rapidly unfolding as the largest combat operation that they had undertaken since the 1991 Gulf War. Saudi tactics in this conflict involved the heavy use of artillery and airpower bombardment followed by the deployment of infantry in mopping up operations. Such tactics were only partially successful as the Houthis proved tough and resilient in the face of bombing and artillery fire. The Saudi army reported that at least 133 of its soldiers were killed in action, with an undisclosed number of others wounded or captured in the fighting.[169] The Saudis discontinued their military involvement in the war in February 2010 when Houthi forces withdrew from Saudi territory, and a cease-fire involving both the Yemeni and Saudi governments was established, with all Saudi prisoners returned. Later, the Houthis gained an important opportunity to assert greater autonomy in their home province of Saada in 2011-12 when the Saleh government was coping with massive domestic unrest across a wide cross section of the Yemeni population.

The 2015 capture of Sana'a by Houthi rebels fighting the Hadi government sent shock waves through the GCC states, although it was initially unclear if the Houthis would seek to hold the city indefinitely or expand their power elsewhere in Yemen. Many of the Arab leaders were concerned about having potentially pro-Iranian Shi'ites in power in Yemen. Most of the conservative Arab leaders have been especially concerned that Houthi clout in Yemen could lead to a wider role for Tehran in the southern Arabian Peninsula. There is no doubt that Iran is providing help to the Houthis, including weapons, but it is a mistake to simply view them as Iranian stooges.[170] As Shi'ites, the Houthis did not expect support from Sunni Arab states during their confrontation with the Yemeni government, and Iran appeared to offer their only option as a strong external ally capable of providing them with material help and political support. Iraq, by contrast, has provided the Houthis with some rhetorical and diplomatic support but nothing more despite its own Shi'ite-led government.[171]

Much like the Iraqi army in Mosul in 2014, the Yemeni army failed to put up a serious defense against the Houthi rebels when they entered Sana'a. The circumstances were somewhat different in this instance than those in Iraq. In Iraq, large elements of the military (especially Sunnis) did not wish to fight for the corrupt, Shi'ite-dominated government of Maliki, and there were also a large number of Iraqi soldiers who were terrified by demonstrated IS brutality. In Yemen, by contrast, much of the army viewed Hadi as weak, and some officers had remained loyal to ousted Saleh. Additionally, Hadi was unpopular with large elements of the public for ending fuel subsidies and more generally failing to improve Yemen's desperate economic situation.[172] Saleh, despite his previous involvement in fighting the Houthis, was now prepared to strike a tactical alliance with them. This sort of duplicity and Machiavellian maneuvering had characterized his 33-year rule and correspondingly cannot be considered a surprise. Before his ouster, Saleh seemed to be preparing his son, Ahmed, to be Yemen's next president.[173] Even after leaving power, he may not have given up on that hope, and many of his supporters openly called for Ahmed's return to run for president.[174] Hadi previously appointed Ahmed as ambassador to the UAE in April 2013 in an effort to remove him from a direct role in Yemeni politics.[175] Hadi then fired Ahmed from that position during his own exile in Saudi Arabia in March 2015, and the UAE correspondingly stripped him of his diplomatic status and privileges.[176]

Hadi fled house arrest in Sana'a in February 2015 and quickly established himself in the southern city of Aden. He clearly hoped to set up a rival center of power there and prove that his presidency was still viable. While Hadi's ability to do this was usually viewed as doubtful, he was able to shore up considerable foreign support, with Saudi Arabia and other Gulf Arab powers moving their embassies to Aden.[177] Hadi's ability to mobilize foreign support for his presidency now seemed a serious threat, and the Houthis began seizing additional territory with the clear strategic goal of eventually capturing Aden. The Houthi movement against Aden triggered Saudi-led military intervention against the Houthis on March 26, 2015. Riyadh gave the United States only a few hours' notice of its impending military actions in Yemen.[178]

Riyadh assembled a 10-nation coalition to participate in the Yemen intervention. Other members of the coalition included Egypt, Jordan, Morocco, Sudan, Pakistan, and all of the GCC countries except Oman.[179] The Pakistani commitment provoked a major domestic backlash, and Islamabad correspondingly never rendered any tangible assistance to the campaign.[180] At the time of this writing, the intervention consists mostly of an air campaign, although some nations, including Saudi Arabia and Egypt, have sent warships off the Yemeni coast and have shelled land targets. The Egyptian government also initially suggested that it was willing to send ground troops to Yemen "if necessary," although it is extremely doubtful they would have ever followed through on this commitment.[181] Limited numbers of Saudi and Emirati forces began fighting in Aden later in the war and have served as leaders of GCC trained and paid Yemeni units that entered Aden by sea, probably from Saudi Arabia and the UAE.[182] Additionally, in late-July 2015, the UAE sent a 1,500 person brigade of its own troops to Aden. This force appeared to be a mechanized infantry unit and has taken some casualties.[183] All of these forces have played an important role in clearing Houthi forces from Aden and surrounding areas.

Almost immediately after the operation began, Washington offered expanded logistical and intelligence support to Saudi Arabia and its regional partners.[184] The United States established a joint coordination and planning cell in the Saudi operations center, and weapons deliveries were also expedited.[185] In April 2015, the Pentagon also announced that the United States was providing aerial refueling for some coalition aircraft. Kerry also warned Iran against efforts to intensify its aid to the Houthis during the fighting. He cited flights coming in from Iran early in the fighting, which he seemed to imply were carrying weapons and war supplies.[186] To underscore the U.S. alliance with Saudi Arabia, Washington sent the aircraft carrier USS *Theodore Roosevelt* and an escort ship to join other U.S. naval ships in the waters off Yemen. The carrier was a reassuring presence to Saudi and Egyptian naval vessels enforcing a newly established UN ban forbidding weapons transfers to the Houthis. Washington may have been especially motived to demonstrate support for Saudi regional concerns following the conclusion of the interim framework agreement on Iranian nuclear issues that proceeded the JCPOA. The Saudis had reluctantly endorsed this agreement, but they had also been extremely concerned about the possibility of such a development for years.[187] They are also deeply uneasy about any agreement that reduces Iran's international isolation and allows it to begin rebuilding its economy, which has been badly racked by sanctions.

The Saudis have stated that they wish to restore Hadi's government, but his internal base of support remains extremely weak. Various militia forces in Aden have fiercely resisted the Houthis whom they view as enemies, but many of these same groups do not support Hadi.[188] Instead, they have fought for anti-Houthi reasons or simply because they do not wish any group representing northern Yemen to have authority in the south. Rather, many would like to see the south restored to its previous status as an independent country.[189] Some reports indicate that Saudi Arabia has also used its embassy in Aden to help organize and fund anti-Houthi tribal fighters, who, as previously noted, can often be significantly more effective than the Yemeni regular army.[190] Nevertheless, these tribal combatants are fighting for money and correspondingly cannot be considered part of Hadi's power base.

The Saudi Arabian Air Force has conducted most of the bombing strikes against Yemeni targets, although Jordan, and especially the UAE, have also participated in some missions.[191] Unsurprisingly, the Saudi-led bombing of Yemen has further damaged relations between the GCC states and Iran. While Riyadh justified the GCC intervention on the basis of supporting the legitimate president, its basic strategic concern was limiting Iranian influence in Yemen. Iran's Supreme Leader, Ayatollah Ali Khamenei called the intervention "genocide" while also asserting that Saudi Arabia is "as bad as Israel."[192] The Iranian leader also stated that "inexperience youths have taken over the affairs of the state and are replacing dignity with barbarity."[193] This was a personal insult to King Salman, who appointed his then-29-year-old son to serve as Saudi Defense Minister in 2015.[194]

The GCC problem with the Houthi rise was compounded by the new AQAP assertiveness in Yemen due to the security vacuum created by the Hadi government's failures. While the GCC would like to prevent Houthi dominance of Yemen, it also wishes to do so in a way that does not benefit AQAP. Since these two forces are fighting each other, they are at least incapable of presenting a united front, although they can do a lot of damage to GCC interests separately.[195] The rise of the Houthis and the collapse of Hadi's already limited authority has also provided AQAP with a variety of opportunities to conduct important large-scale operations within Yemen. In one particularly dramatic development on April 2, 2015, AQAP fighters stormed a prison in Hadramaut Province and freed 300 prisoners, including many of their imprisoned comrades.[196] On July 1, 2015, an even more alarming jail break took place when 1,200 prisoners were reported to have been freed from the central prison in the city of Taiz.[197] An undisclosed number of these prisoners are AQAP members or supporters.[198] In early 2015, AQAP was also able to seize and control territory including the port of Mukallah, Yemen's fifth largest city, although it had worked together with local officials and tribes in a possible attempt to prove that it is no longer interested in implementing the types of brutality associated with previous AQAP control of Yemeni territory.[199] The Houthis sometimes maintain that AQAP will seize any land that they relinquish control over as part of a peace agreement.

Despite the importance of AQAP in Yemen, there is a limited but expanding role by Yemeni associates of the Islamic State organization. On March 20, 2015, fighters claiming to be associated with IS conducted their first major operation in Yemen using suicide bombers to attack a number of Shi'ite mosques, killing 142 people and wounding more than 350. A few days later, a newly announced "Green Brigade" asserting IS ties claimed to have killed a few Houthis in the central province of Ibb.[200] Since that time a number of skirmishes have taken place between Yemeni or Houthi soldiers and fighters claiming an IS affiliation. Mosques utilized by Shi'ites have remained a favored IS target.[201]

A potential advantage for AQAP and IS supporters in Yemen is the crippling of U.S.-Yemeni counterterrorism cooperation. The United States has withdrawn

125 Special Forces trainers and other U.S. personnel from Yemen as it has descended into chaos.[202] Washington has also withdrawn its embassy from Sana'a and relocated the U.S. diplomatic mission to Jeddah, Saudi Arabia.[203] This move enormously complicates counterterrorism coordination with both the Yemeni government institutions that remain in that country and the Yemeni military. These conditions have not ended drone use, although the potential for collateral damage with armed drones is virtually always enhanced by the lack of accurate intelligence obtained by friendly forces on the ground.[204] Without such intelligence, the United States has been reported to have been forced to rely on "signature strikes" against AQAP targets in Yemen. Signature strikes involve selecting targets based on observed patterns of behavior rather than precise information on the identity of targeted personnel.[205] Despite their controversial nature, these efforts have sometimes yielded important results, as when a June 2015 drone strike killed AQAP chief Nasir al-Wuhayshi.[206]

It is difficult to envision the Yemeni war going on indefinitely without creating a massive humanitarian crisis. Yemen was a desperately poor country even before the fighting began, and it now faces the danger of large amounts of people being unable to access food and uncontaminated drinking water. Diseases are spreading throughout the country, and large scale epidemics appear possible.[207] While the Saudi leadership detests the Houthis to the point that serious diplomatic progress with them does not seem likely, Riyadh is more willing to negotiate with former President Saleh, who is also a key part of the conflict.[208] The strong position of the Hadi government in Aden also improves the Saudi negotiating position and may help the Saudis reach an overall agreement. It is not, however, clear if Yemen will emerge from this crisis as one or two countries. It is fully possible that an independent south will re-emerge from this crisis and will align strongly with Riyadh.

U.S. Defense Ties with the Gulf Arab States.

In addressing the threats that they currently face, Arab allies must balance domestic public opinion with defense needs. Many Arab states have maintained a long and problematic history with Western military bases on their territory, and this background influences current Gulf Arab decisionmaking on how to organize military cooperation with the United States. Until at least the 1950s, great powers often maintained that their bases were designed to defend regional nations against foreign invaders, but the presence of such facilities was sometimes used to pressure and influence local governments. In response to these concerns, as well as changing Western military requirements and economic pressures, Western permanent military presence in the Middle East steadily declined, and a number of major bases were evacuated in response to nationalist demands. By the early-1970s, the United States and other Western nations had dramatically scaled down their presence in the area. Western combat units currently retain an ongoing presence at military facilities only in some smaller Gulf Arab states including Bahrain, Kuwait, Qatar, and the UAE. In Jordan, the United States maintains hundreds of military personnel in that country to prepare for the large and important Eager Lion exercise (discussed later). The U.S. Army also stationed significant forces in Saudi Arabia during and after Operations DESERT

SHIELD and DESERT STORM in 1990-91, but these forces were withdrawn in 2003. Iraqi bases host U.S. advisors and planners (along with some force protection units) but not U.S. Army or Marine Corps maneuver combat units.

Most of the Gulf Arab countries traditionally have not favored large numbers of ground forces permanently stationed on their territory, and some have shown a preference for air or naval bases. Western facilities in Bahrain support the U.S. Fifth Fleet, while Qatar and the UAE allow the U.S. Air Force to utilize key air bases, although only a limited number of U.S. aircraft regularly use these facilities. Many of the U.S. combat aircraft currently used to protect the Gulf are naval aircraft stationed on aircraft carriers, although the U.S. Air Force presence in the region can be expanded in emergency situations. Conversely, Kuwait has a much more extensive history of hosting both U.S. ground and air forces, with many U.S. Army troops being stationed at Camp Arifjan, south of Kuwait city.[209] Currently, Camp Arifjan is an important transit point for equipment being returned to the United States from Afghanistan. At this time, around 13,500 U.S. service members are stationed in Kuwait, down from 25,000 during the last stages of the U.S. military presence in Iraq.[210] Around 40,000 U.S. military personnel of all services are deployed to the Middle East (mostly the Gulf) at any one time.

Military Exercises.

Large military exercises have been somewhat less prominent over the last few years as ongoing wars in the region have required the attention of both the United States and its regional partners. A number of

Arab air forces have been engaged in air combat operations as part of the struggles in Iraq, Syria, and Yemen. Some Arab naval forces, including those of Egypt and Saudi Arabia, also may have been marginally involved in the fighting in Yemen. Limited numbers of Saudi and Emirati ground forces have also fought in Yemen, as noted earlier. Yet, if joint U.S.-Arab military exercises have been somewhat overshadowed by actual combat recently, they nevertheless remain important to all parties. One of the most important advantages of military exercises is that some Arab countries, which display reticence about large numbers of foreign ground troops being stationed permanently on their soil, seek other forms of cooperation with U.S. military forces. The decision to reduce significantly U.S. Army forces in Europe from Cold War levels is also widely understood to complicate U.S. power projection into the Middle East by moving troops farther away, although that trend may eventually be reversed. The 2014-15 difficulties in Ukraine, Crimea, and elsewhere in Eastern Europe may lead to a significant upward revision of the optimal numbers of U.S. forces in Europe. Currently, such actions appear to be confined mostly to pre-positioning weapons and equipment, including M1A2 tanks and M2A3/M3A3 Bradley infantry fighting vehicles, for use of military exercises or other training.[211]

Throughout the Middle East, many Arab countries are extremely interested in working with the U.S. military in joint exercises to help them continue professionalizing their armed forces and raising their standards for conventional defense, joint operations, intelligence operations, counterinsurgency, and other capabilities. U.S. commitment to support these activities through both training and exercises is clearly reassuring to friendly Arab states that are seeking to warn their enemies against aggressive action. To help meet these concerns, former Secretary of Defense Chuck Hagel made a number of visits to the region and also made a number of strong statements about the continuing U.S. interest in the region. In December 2013, he gave a particularly important speech at a conference in Manama, Bahrain, designed to underscore the future U.S. commitment to the partnership with Gulf allies. Hagel acknowledged that Arab allies were concerned over the U.S. decision to rebalance forces to Asia and cuts to the U.S. Defense budget, but insisted that these changes did not mean the abandonment of the Middle East. Hagel then envisioned a U.S. military presence of around 35,000 personnel and a U.S. Army footprint of 10,000 troops in the region.[212] These numbers are somewhat larger now with around 40,000 military personnel in the Middle East at any one time.[213] Hagel also noted that the United States maintained around 40 ships at sea in the region including an aircraft carrier battle group. Defense Secretary Ashton Carter has also embraced these policies when he replaced Hagel.[214]

In this environment, many friendly Arab political and military leaders have found U.S.-led bilateral or multinational military exercises to be an exceptionally valuable tool for their security. Exercises, unlike basing rights, do not involve a long-term military presence that can grate on domestic public opinion and provide the appearance of excessive U.S. influence. Rather, military exercises can more easily be portrayed as a collaboration, in which the United States is showing its support for local militaries by working with them. Another advantage is that at times of domestic Arab political tension, exercises can usually be rescheduled by the host government. Conversely, at times of regional tension, regularly scheduled exercises can be expanded and the number of U.S. troops participating in the exercise can be increased to show support for the host government. Such expansions are generally seen in the region as a show of force, although their linkage to previously planned exercises allows the United States and its allies to deny that they are being provocative. Exercise Eager Lion, which is based in Jordan and involves the United States and a number of Gulf Arab allies, may be an example of this approach. Also, as a result of the July 2015 JCPOA, the United States is considering increasing the scope and number of multilateral exercises in the Gulf as a way of reassuring regional allies.[215]

Another reason for a vigorous ongoing U.S.-Gulf exercise program involves Iranian actions. The Iranians frequently engage in large-scale joint exercises, which they use for both training and propaganda purposes. The land component of these exercises is usually defensive, focusing on responding to a U.S.-led invasion of the Iranian homeland, which appears to be one of their primary military concerns. The Iranians usually proclaim these exercises to be completely successful and routinely exaggerate the numbers of forces involved, although the exercises remain meaningful as political theater.[216] U.S.-led maritime exercises include not only large units, but also smaller ships. Multinational military exercises focused on anti-mining operations are particularly important since mine warfare is an important part of Iran's maritime strategy that, as with land forces, stresses asymmetric capabilities.[217] As with landpower and airpower, Iran is totally outclassed by allied capabilities at sea and therefore will continue to develop asymmetric capabilities in areas such as submarine warfare, mine warfare, and the use of fast small armed boats.

The centerpiece of the Middle Eastern military exercise program was formerly Exercise Bright Star, held in Egypt. Unless cancelled for political or military reasons, Egypt has previously hosted Bright Star every 2 years. Bright Star exercises began in 1980 following the conclusion of the 1979 Egyptian-Israeli peace treaty, with the most recent exercise occurring in October 2009. This exercise has served as a large, multinational training exercise that helps foster the interoperability of U.S., Egyptian, and allied forces. Bright Star eventually became the most important U.S. supported military exercise in the Middle East and a showpiece of U.S.-Egyptian military cooperation. It was cancelled in 2003 due to U.S. commitments to the wars in Iraq and Afghanistan. It was cancelled again in 2011 due to the Egyptian revolution and in 2013 due to U.S. concerns about the ouster of Morsi by the military. The outlook for this exercise therefore appears to be uncertain for the foreseeable future due primarily to U.S.-Egyptian differences over human rights as well as Egypt's focus on suppressing a very serious insurgency within its borders. Nevertheless, in early August 2015, Kerry stated that the United States and Egypt were moving toward resuming Bright Star, although details about any progress in this effort have not been made public.[218]

While never directly presented overseas as a replacement for Bright Star, the Jordanian-based Exercise Eager Lion has been conducted for 5 consecutive years since 2011 (twice as often as Bright Star under its normal circumstances). Exercise Eager Lion has grown out of the earlier and smaller Exercise Infinite Moonlight, which began in 1996 and continued until the establishment of Eager Lion, with some interruptions because of the U.S.-led invasion of Iraq. This earlier bilateral exercise centered on the strong participation of the U.S. Marine Corps and focused primarily on Jordanian security rather than wider regional concerns. In the future, it will be possible for the conservative Arab states to expand their limited participation in Eager Lion exercises due to the uncertain status of the Egyptian-based Bright Star exercises.

Eager Lion has an especially robust landpower component, which is important for U.S-Arab cooperation. In many Arab states, the army is the dominant service, and in all Arab countries, it is an important military service, so coordination with Arab ground forces will be especially important. In only a few wealthy Arab states such as Saudi Arabia, has the air force been more favored historically (primarily due to air force requirements for fewer human resources and a belief that armies rather than air forces can more effectively conduct anti-government coups). All of the Gulf States have small navies that function primarily as coastal defense forces, but U.S. Navy joint exercises with Arab navies are important due to the need to defend the numerous strategic waterways in the region. They will probably never involve the level of U.S.-Arab coordination and cooperation as exercises involving landpower, although the large joint U.S. military presence is vital for the defense of the region.[219]

Many observers believe Eager Lion also sends a message of solidarity with Jordan at a time of immense concern over Syria and Iraq. The message might have been reinforced by the U.S. decision to leave a Patriot missile battery and a limited number of F-16 fighter aircraft behind for use in future exercises.[220] Since Eager Lion 2013, about 700-900 U.S. Army and Air Force personnel remained in Jordan to support these systems, along with around 100 soldiers stationed there throughout the year as a forward headquarters of the 1st Armored Division.[221] Although Jordan is not a Gulf State, it is an Arab monarchy which works extremely closely with both the Gulf Arabs and the United States on regional security matters. Ongoing Gulf participation in large multinational Eager Lion exercises may send an additional important message of U.S.-Gulf solidarity. The Gulf States are also involved in numerous smaller bilateral exercises with the United States within their own territory as well as the GCC's Peninsula Shield exercises.[222]

The Importance of Regionally Aligned Forces.

In addition to military exercises, such as Eager Lion, one potentially effective way of improving U.S. landpower coordination with its Arab allies is through Regionally Aligned Forces (RAFs). RAFs units are a U.S. Army initiative based on the lessons of the Iraq and Afghanistan wars as well as earlier efforts to prepare U.S. Army units to fight in various regions. Aspects of the RAFs initiative are still undergoing evaluation and may be subject to ongoing modification over time. The concept involves U.S. Army maneuver combat units and their support forces being focused on a specific Geographic Combatant Command region as part of their normal training program.[223] This concept was initially tested with a program to prepare the first such brigade for service with Africa Command, where it was successful enough to be considered a model for the Army component of the other Geographic Combatant Commands.

RAFs units are expected to incorporate militarily useful information about the regions on which they are focused into planning and training. This approach is partially enabled through interaction with their counterparts from friendly regional countries. These units are expected to receive cultural training and language familiarization for the areas where they might be required to operate. By working more closely with regional militaries on a recurring basis, U.S. personnel are expected to interface quickly and effectively with their counterparts during an escalating crisis. Ideally, the soldiers of each nation will gain a working knowledge of the other states' Standard Operating Procedures (SOPs) and establish good working relationships with their counterparts in partner military forces. Additionally, the U.S. Army and partner militaries seek to establish a common understanding of key military considerations that would enhance their ability to train and fight effectively together. Cooperation with local forces also has been strongly enhanced by the presence of numerous officers from allied nations who have received training and military education in the United States. An additional advantage is that English is widely spoken by officers in most Gulf militaries and some other militaries (such as that of Jordan) within the larger Middle East.

A central idea of the RAFs is that by gaining an enhanced understanding of the area, these units will avoid a "cold start" in actual military operations and identify avoidable mistakes in coordination, communications, and planning early in the process.[224] The projected reduction in U.S. Army division, corps, and Army Service Component Command staffs by 25 percent will make such efficiencies especially important in future operations.[225] Subjects of military utility include cultures and subcultures (including ethnic and religious minorities); rural and urban geography (especially infrastructure); relevant languages; and the organization, doctrine, and effectiveness of partner militaries. The expense of such programs is somewhat mitigated by the fact that not every maneuver combat unit needs to be aligned with a Geographic Combat Command, but even limited expertise could be useful.[226] General Raymond Odierno's political advisor in Iraq, Emma Sky, has provided some insight on this problem, noting that U.S. forces entered the country with a deeply oversimplified view of the potential for conflict in Iraq once Saddam had been removed. In general terms, she felt that too many officers simply assumed that the only serious potential for violence was fighting between die-hard Baathists and newly liberated Iraqis. Sky maintains that U.S. military forces were slow in understanding the ethnic and sectarian problems that might arise from other sources such as intensified conflict between the Sunni and Kurdish populations, the area in which she was stationed early in the war.[227] A greater awareness of these types of problems could be especially useful during any future rapidly evolving conflict that includes U.S. military participation.

A potential problem with RAFs is the difficulty and expense of soldiers gaining reasonable proficiency in some skills associated with the concept. Gaining an in-depth cultural knowledge of the region including key differences between various sub-cultures is often difficult, but even a limited amount of knowledge on such subjects can be useful if the limited scope of this knowledge is fully understood. In contrast, language proficiency is almost always the most difficult of RAFs-related skills to master, often being expensive and time consuming.[228] Even a basic proficiency in Arabic or other Middle Eastern languages can never be gained in the pre-deployment courses of 8 or 16 weeks, since these languages are extraordinarily difficult for Westerners to learn. Soldiers encountering unfamiliar local dialects would also have serious problems in communicating, even if they have been given more comprehensive language study. A further problem is that much of the language training is not maintained for soldiers that are rotated back to the United States and then redeployed at a later date.[229] Noting these shortcomings, there is still value in providing language familiarization to soldiers, but the limitation of this effort is important to understand. Basic words and phrases can sometimes be of considerably more value than knowing nothing about a language. Additionally, in many cultures and often in the Middle East, local people seem to genuinely appreciate efforts by U.S. personnel to use their language. Under these circumstances, language familiarization remains important to RAF units.

Cultural and linguistic knowledge also has value for other reasons than warfighting. Often U.S. military forces extensively interact with civilian populations as part of both warfighting and in a post-conflict environment. Sometimes they are asked to work with civilians to a much greater extent than they ever expected, such as in the aftermath of the 2003 invasion of Iraq. At this time, many U.S. officers believed that their forces would be replaced or at least supplemented by what Sky and her associates were told would be "a rapidly deployable team of experts with resources and ready-made systems."[230] The shorthand for this concept was "government in a box," which never came, despite the promises given to the U.S. military about nongovernmental organizations and other forms of civilian support. These people, not the military, were expected to address the majority of problems involving non-security issues with the civilian population. Sky sarcastically describes the entire concept as a "mythical" rather than a "magical" concept, much to the disappointment of many soldiers, who saw such activities as completely different from their primary mission of warfighting.[231]

Currently, some of the aspects of the RAFs concept are being addressed in meaningful ways by large and important units. The 1st Armored Division, based in Fort Bliss, Texas, has been aligned with U.S. Central Command (CENTCOM) and has played an important role in the Eager Lion exercises previously discussed.[232] During various Eager Lion exercises, the 1st Armored Division provided the bulk of the U.S. Army ground forces assigned to the exercise. As part of the alignment with CENTCOM, 1st Armored Division has assisted the Jordanians with integrated missile defense, humanitarian assistance, and disaster relief.[233] A strong working relationship with Jordan is particularly useful since forces operating out of this country can move into the Gulf area quickly if they are needed. The presence of such forces at times of crisis in the Gulf could be a restraining influence on potential aggressors. Adding to these advantages, the King Abdullah II Special Operations Training Center (KASOTC), about 20 kilometers northeast of Amman, has also been proven to be an excellent command and control site for combined U.S.-Jordanian operations.[234]

The Challenges of Building Partner Capacity and Sharing the Lessons of Counterinsurgency.

The concept of building partner capacity has undergone serious setbacks in mid-2014 due to the catastrophic military problems suffered by both the Iraqi and Yemeni armies at that time. The United States had strong train and equip programs for each of these countries in the past, and the program for Yemen was ongoing when the Yemeni military fragmented in September 2014.[235] Additionally, harsher critics maintain that the Iraqi Army is too corrupt to assume the challenges of a serious military force, pointing to such problems as officer kickbacks and "ghost soldiers," who receive salaries (usually pocketed by their officers) and have their names on personnel rosters but do not serve in units.[236] There is also the question of how much can be accomplished by training foreign soldiers serving in countries with corrupt civilian and military elites. In a forceful statement on this problem, former Deputy Director of the Central Intelligence Agency (CIA) John McLaughlin said, "People don't fight because they've been trained; they fight because they believe in something. At present, the biggest believers in the region are with the Islamic State."[237] These problems indicate that train and equip programs, while important, will not work well in instances where governments are widely viewed as illegitimate by significant elements of their population and officer corps are involved in excessive corruption.

The wars in Afghanistan and Iraq have reinforced the understanding that counterinsurgencies often can take years, if not decades, to resolve. These operations require time, public patience, and significant numbers of troops trained in counterinsurgency tactics. These troops optimally should be provided by the government rather than an outside power. Air and naval forces can play important supporting roles in counterinsurgencies, but ground forces almost always have to take the lead. Armed drones have also played an important role in countries such as Yemen, but strike weapons can only address certain aspects of the insurgent problem. They can kill insurgents but cannot reassert government authority in contested areas. It is therefore important that U.S. Army forces continue to provide practical advice and assistance to friendly nations, while maintaining as light a footprint as possible in those countries where military reform is possible and enabled by political reform.[238]

The U.S. Army and Marine Corps learned a great deal during the fighting in Iraq that may be useful for addressing other Middle Eastern insurgencies. While no two conflicts are alike, it is possible that some could have value in addressing the insurgencies that currently exist in a number of Middle Eastern countries including U.S. allies such as Egypt and Yemen. GCC states also view both of these insurgencies as dangerous, but they are most clearly focused on the future of Yemen.[239] Currently, the GCC states, especially Saudi Arabia, are more focused on removing the Houthis from power, which they view as a prerequisite for moving against AQAP. Although AQAP was defeated and lost overt control of the contested territory in 2012, it remained a strong terrorist and insurgent force and never gave up on the idea of creating an al-Qaeda emirate in southern Yemen, which could become a threat to Saudi Arabia and other Gulf States.[240] The 2015 capture of the city of Mukallah, discussed earlier, is clearly an effort in that direction. In the long term, AQAP can probably only be eradicated by a reformed

Yemeni army that fights effectively and avoids large-scale corruption. Moreover, Yemeni troops that are inadequately trained for counterinsurgency can take significant casualties and make serious mistakes that harm the struggle against AQAP. Fortunately, at least some Yemeni senior officers are also deeply committed to improving the quality of the force.[241]

The Iraqi government faces a hybrid war which involves significant elements of conventional and insurgent warfare. Sectarian hatreds are also a powerful component of this war. IS is directing acts of terrorism against government facilities and institutions as well as Shi'ite citizens in partial response to Sunni grievances but also to advance the IS agenda. The U.S. leadership will therefore have to make decisions on how to help the Iraqi government with advice and military equipment, while pushing it to be more inclusive and less corrupt.[242] A key to any successful counterinsurgency is to place distance between the insurgents and the population where they operate. The Iraqi government cannot do this if it only serves the interest of its Shi'ite citizens. U.S. Army training and other support correspondingly must be closely linked to political reform, but military aid is vital and optimally effective once the Iraqi government moves forward in a serious effort at reform and Sunni inclusion.

Some important lessons of the Iraq War that may be of the most interest to local forces are tactical. This conflict involved a great deal of trial and error efforts by deployed troops, who, over time, developed new forms of "best practices" for the conduct of counterinsurgencies in Iraq and Afghanistan. In an excellent study of these issues, James A. Russell of the U.S. Naval Postgraduate School notes that, in these circumstances, doctrine is only a general guide, and that the operational environment ultimately has a tremendous impact on mission requirements.[243] U.S. troops also encountered relatively unexpected problems that they found limited and more comprehensive solutions for over time. New tactics, techniques, and procedures were developed as well as new and more flexible SOPs.[244] In one especially interesting insight, Russell notes that random searches of houses were regarded by the Iraqis as harassment, and this problem hurt U.S. military relations with the population. In Ramadi, however, patrol leaders came up with a highly innovative solution whereby affected citizens were provided with gifts of small toys, candy, and several two-pound bags of sugar to help reduce the anger over such visits.[245]

Intelligence, Counterintelligence, and Counterterrorism Support.

Intelligence support is one of the forms of U.S. assistance that is most often requested by Arab states.[246] Many Arab leaders consider U.S. intelligence information both useful and a sufficiently low profile form of cooperation that will not usually excite nationalist anger. Such support is especially helpful in dealing with insurgent groups such as IS and Yemen's Houthis which can field large military formations. Some Arab countries such as Jordan have excellent intelligence organizations, but they also have little choice except to rely heavily on the use of human agents. The gap in their capabilities usually involves the technical intelligence gathering that the United States is often considered to do very well. Arab governments concerned about foreign-sponsored subversion and terrorism often view efficient intelligence organizations as vital to their well-being and perhaps even survival. While the use of armed drones against terrorists tends to dominate headlines, unarmed drones are also an important source of military intelligence for the United States and its allies and may be particularly useful in counterinsurgency actions. According to the *Defense News*, the United States was flying about 50 intelligence gathering drone missions a day over Iraq in July 2014 in the aftermath of the seizure of northern Iraq by IS.[247]

The United States can also provide technical support to allied militaries including helping to protect friendly command and control systems and the provision of cyber security technologies. Apart from battlefield counterintelligence, many Arab states are also deeply concerned about IS, al-Qaeda, and other radical cells operating within the civilian population of their countries. These allies seek U.S. support and information sharing to deal with internal terrorist activity. The problem became exceptionally serious in instances where powerful al-Qaeda affiliates have sprung up as a side effect of the Syrian civil war. Al-Nusra and the Islamic State are difficult to classify as pure terrorism and guerrilla warfare organizations since they also practice conventional warfare. Correspondingly, the Gulf States have also openly worried about "sleeper cells" in their countries that either serve al-Qaeda and its allies or those that might carry out acts of terrorism on the orders of Iran or Lebanese Hezbollah.[248] Many states are also interested in U.S. technical help in securing their borders from terrorist infiltration.[249] The potential problem here is that U.S. officials want to help these nations defeat terrorists, but they also have to be careful to ensure that such intelligence is not misused to strike at legitimate political opposition forces or groups targeted for ethnic or sectarian reasons.

Air and Missile Defense.

Many Arab states, especially those of the GCC, are concerned about the extensive and formidable Iranian surface-to-surface missile program.[250] U.S. defense officials have stated that the United States is aware of the Gulf States' anxieties about Iranian missiles and that the United States is determined to support them in building a coordinated missile defense capability.[251] The most important components of this layered defense are the Patriot air and missile defense system and the Terminal High Altitude Area Defense system (THAAD). Many partner countries within the region already have Patriot systems and have or are now acquiring PAC-3 anti-missile capabilities for those systems. The United States has also rapidly moved to increase the sale of PAC-3 missiles to Saudi Arabia following the conclusion of the JCPOA with Iran and support to other GCC nations is expected to increase as well.[252] The UAE has made THAAD purchases and delivery is expected to begin in late-2015.[253] Saudi Arabia and Qatar are also expected to purchase THAAD systems.[254] With so much at stake, these states are tremendously interested in working with the United States on missile defense.

Surface-to-surface missiles (such as Scuds) have been used extensively in some Middle Eastern wars, although they have never been employed with unconventional (chemical, biological, or nuclear) warheads. In the Gulf area, conflicts involving surface-to-surface missiles include attacks made by both sides during the Iran-Iraq war and missile strikes against Saudi targets during Operation DESERT STORM.[255] Saddam Hussein also reached outside of the Gulf area and fired 39 extended range Scud missiles at Israel during the 1991 conflict, although there were very few Israeli casualties. Elsewhere in the Middle East, Scud missiles were used by secessionist forces in Yemen during the 1994 civil war, and there have been some reports of Syrian government forces occasionally firing Scuds at rebel forces early in Syria's civil war.[256] One Scud missile was apparently fired at Saudi Arabia by Houthi forces in 2015 but was then believed to have been shot down by a Saudi Patriot missile. Iran also has an extensive program of missile development that is much more sophisticated than the Scuds used in various Middle Eastern wars. Iran is a large country, and many of Iran's longer range missiles can be located in remote parts of the country and still strike the Gulf Arab countries and would be much more difficult to reach and target with airpower than the shorter range Scuds.

Friendly Gulf military forces are extremely interested in additional systems to defend their airspace against air and missile strikes because of the significant resources that Iran has applied to its ballistic missile program and the fear that Iranian missiles will eventually be armed with unconventional warheads.[257] In any scenario where Iranian missiles are fired at a Gulf State, one might reasonably expect that U.S. and Gulf air forces will seek to destroy as many of these systems on the ground as possible. Such actions are indispensable, but there are continuing questions about how long this will take. The last U.S. war against an enemy which was well-armed with missiles occurred in 1991 in Iraq. At that time, Saddam Hussein's forces were able to fire a number of Scuds and modified Scuds at coalition military forces and Israel despite a substantial air campaign to destroy these assets.

The United States has sometimes pushed the GCC states to consider ways of improving the level of integration of their missile defense systems. Hagel served as the driving force behind a 2013 initiative allowing the GCC to purchase missile defense systems as a bloc, and then integrate their radars, sensors, and early warning systems.[258] This approach did not go forward due to distrust among individual GCC members. Nevertheless, such efforts cannot be abandoned if these countries are to optimize their defense. Moreover, a truly integrated missile defense program will require a high level of agreement among members about such issues as rules of engagement and coordination. Leading U.S. defense expert Anthony H. Cordesman notes that "You have to work out the entire engagement structure before the first missile is ever launched."[259]

Conclusions.

1. **U.S. leaders need to be aware that Arab attitudes on their military ties with the United States have changed since the 2003-11 Iraq War**. While many Arabs formerly believed U.S. policies into the Middle East were too intrusive into their region, this attitude is now less prevalent. Rather, many friendly Arab leaders believe that the United States is no longer as interested in strong military links to their countries due to its experiences with war in Iraq and Afghanistan. Arab states need to be reassured by both words and actions that any new defense emphasis on Asia or elsewhere is not to be conducted at their expense.

2. **The United States must be aware of the increased concerns that Saudi Arabia and other Arab states have about Iran**. Saudi Arabia and various

other Arab states detested Saddam Hussein but had always hoped that he would be replaced by a friendly Sunni strongman. The Saudis were not interested in either a democratic Iraq or a Shi'ite-dominated Iraq. Now Saudi leaders feel that Iraq has ceased to be a bulwark against Iran and is instead a quasi-ally of Iran. This development represents a significant change in the balance of power which the Saudis and some of their Arab allies believe is being played out in a more aggressive foreign policy, including Iranian assertiveness on Bahrain and Yemen as well as Iraq. While some of these concerns sound excessive to Western ears, they are very real to many Arabs and must be treated with respect. Nevertheless, if U.S. relations with Iran improve dramatically (which is doubtful in the short term), then that development will probably result from conditions that will also allow for Arab states to improve their relations with Iran.

3. **Closely related to the previous point, the United States must continue to emphasize that any improvement in relations with Iran will not come at the expense of other Middle Eastern allies**. A dramatic improvement in such relations remains uncertain and the question of Iranian nuclear development is still unclear. If the JCPOA negotiated by the P5+1 is successful, then questions will arise over how the global community will interact with Iran in the future. Under no circumstances should the United States appear to support an Iranian position of dominance in the region, but it should also be willing to improve relations with Iran if the regime backs away from some of its most repugnant policies. A key point here is that the GCC states, Jordan, and even Egypt will continue to depend upon the United States, and, to a lesser

extent, the UK, to keep their militaries operational. Limited and symbolic acts of cooperation with other suppliers such as France and Russia can do little to change this reality. The United States must therefore carefully discuss its plans for future polices on Iran with these states, but it cannot give them a veto over U.S. policy initiatives.

4. **The United States must continue arms sales to friendly Arab states concerned about Iran, but cannot assume that relations will be harmonious because of these sales**. Arab states buy military equipment from the United States both to modernize their military forces and to consolidate relations with the United States. If UN and other restrictions on arms sales to Iran are eventually lifted as envisioned in the Iranian nuclear agreement or if loopholes develop in the future, these states will need more support.

5. **The Strategy of "train and equip" or "arm and train" for Arab allies needs to be retained but cannot be treated as a panacea for Middle East security problems. Instead, it must be used in specific situations where the United States objectively assesses foreign soldiers to be both trainable and motivated**. After setbacks in Iraq and Yemen, it is now clear that unmotivated officers and soldiers sometimes permeate allied militaries and cannot be depended upon to fight regardless of how much effort is dedicated to providing them with modern weapons and training. To make matters worse, such soldiers may repeat the 2014 Mosul example and abandon massive amounts of weapons and equipment to enemy forces. In future scenarios, friendly forces receiving such training must be evaluated continuously and honestly regarding

their levels of motivation, and this information must be collated and passed on to senior military leaders. U.S. officials must make assessments of friendly troops' vulnerabilities to enemy psychological warfare and the ways in which national government graft and corruption filter into the military and cause a breakdown of government legitimacy. It needs to be well understood that a national military is usually no better than the government it is asked to defend and efforts at government reform must be pressed. The alternative to this approach cannot be allowed to become having U.S. forces fight the battles for these troops and leave dysfunctional, unreformed militaries in place. The United States should be willing to play a supporting military role in helping regional allies and not attempt to Americanize every conflict.

6. **Closely related to the point noted previously, the United States must recognize that buying time for threatened regimes through airpower or drones can only be successful if the time is used well as an opportunity to raise the warfighting capabilities of the militaries (especially the ground forces) of the country under siege and improve the quality of government to give soldiers something for which to fight**. Otherwise, you may be simply postponing the inevitable collapse of a weak and often illegitimate government with a military that cannot defend it. All Middle Eastern states do not have to evolve into Western-style democracies, but many need to reduce dysfunctional levels of corruption and begin to provide some basic fairness in the political process and the administration of justice. Drone strikes, including "decapitation strikes" that kill terrorist leaders, can create setbacks for the organizations challenging weak governments,

but new leaders will always be found to replace them. Drones, by themselves, do not win wars.

7. **The United States and its allies may have to accept some limited tacit cooperation with the Assad regime in Syria in order to destroy or at least weaken IS in that country**. This is not an easy recommendation to make or to follow. The Assad regime is responsible for the deaths of hundreds of thousands of Syrians and has conducted warfare against civilians as well as anti-regime fighters. One of the only virtues that the Assad regime possesses is that IS is worse. The Egyptians and more recently the Jordanians seem to understand this situation. The GCC states may come to this conclusion eventually since IS is a direct threat to them and Assad is not. This tacit cooperation could involve such steps as more coalition efforts to bomb assembly areas for jihadists preparing to strike regime strongholds. In the highly unlikely event that Syrian moderates can be propped up to the point that they become a serious force in the war, this may allow the United States and its Arab allies more options. Nevertheless, Syrian moderates (except for Syrian Kurds) are not a force in that country now, and it is increasingly difficult to generate any reality-based scenario of how they might come to power. The United States may, nevertheless, have to continue supporting Syrian moderate fighters for political reasons to help prove that the United States is not biased against Sunni Arabs eventually taking power in Syria by ousting the Alawite-led regime.

8. **The United States needs to support a fair and timely settlement of the crisis in Yemen. A Yemen in chaos is not in the interests of the United States,**

and the U.S. military needs to be able to return to the mission of helping the Yemeni military, or at least their elite forces, deal with threats such as AQAP and IS, not the Houthis. The Houthi coup, backed by ex-President Saleh, was unwise and has led to terrible consequences. Nevertheless, not all Houthi claims are illegitimate, and giving them a more equitable stake in the Yemeni future is a good idea. In particular, Houthis in their home province of Saada should not be subject to excessive harassment by Salafi missionaries or militias, and they should receive a fair share of development aid. It is true that the Houthis are receiving aid, including military aid, from the Iranians, but at the present time they see that as their only option for a tolerable future in Yemen. A political solution therefore appears possible. Additionally, if the war in Yemen continues to drag on, it is imperative for the United States to continue stressing the need to get humanitarian relief to that country.

9. **To the extent possible, the United States should retain a strong intelligence gathering where friendly governments may be threatened.** This is the form of support that these regimes most often support. Nevertheless, U.S. military intelligence personnel need to be aware that some technology and training used for counterterrorism can also be used for suppressing legitimate dissent. If U.S. support is being misused, this problem needs to be quickly and clearly conveyed to senior military leaders who must then pass it on to the U.S. civilian leadership.

10. **The U.S. military leadership must continue to emphasize a vigorous military exercise program.** Organizing the timing, scope, and mix of forces for these

exercises can be calibrated to meet regional threats while showing appropriate respect for the equality and sovereignty of U.S. partners in the region. Eager Lion is clearly a major success and should be continued.

11. **The U.S. Army should continue to emphasize the value of RAFs.** In the face of growing threats, many partner nations are almost certain to welcome U.S. support in providing RAFs acting in multilateral exercises to help improve their military performance in such skills as air and missile defense, chemical and biological protection, counterinsurgency operations, intelligence, and other important aspects of multilateral military cooperation.

12. **Military forces (including RAFs) working with Middle Eastern and Gulf militaries will need to be properly supported with personnel, material resources, and funding for the ongoing training with counterpart militaries.** If these units receive fewer resources than units aligned to the Pacific, this will be noticed by both Gulf allies and potential adversaries. The U.S. Government emphasis on the Pacific is important but cannot be allowed to seriously weaken other commands or bring our commitment to key allies into question.

13. **The United States must continue to support missile defense by those nations that feel most threatened by Iran.** This is another central concern to GCC states and must be treated as a key priority for both symbolic and military purposes.

ENDNOTES

1. See, for example, Daniel C. Kurter, Scott B. Lasensky, William B. Quandt, Steven L. Speigel, and Shelby Telhami, *The Peace Puzzle: America's Quest for Arab-Israeli Peace, 1989-2011*, Ithaca, NY: Cornell University Press, 2013.

2. For an overview of past Presidential priorities and policies toward the Middle East, see Patrick Tyler, *A World of Trouble: The White House and the Middle East from the Cold War to the War on Terror*, New York: Farrar, Straus and Giroux, 2009.

3. Office of the White House Press Secretary, "Remarks by the President on the Middle East and North Africa," Washington, DC: The White House, May 19, 2011, available from *www.whitehouse.gov*, accessed March 1, 2013. In this speech, Obama also spoke about the advancement of democracy and human rights but did not explicitly name them as core interests.

4. Lalit K. Jha, "Gulf Region Remains Important for US Interest: Dempsey," *Press Trust of India*, March 19, 2013.

5. "The Economics of shale oil," *Economist*, February 15, 2014, p. 23.

6. On the importance of Gulf Oil exports for the world economy and the requirement for military forces to prevent the disruption of their export during certain scenarios, see Kenneth Katzman, *et al.*, *Iran's Threat to the Strait of Hormuz*, Washington DC: Congressional Research Service, 2012, pp. 13-15; David Crist, *The Twilight War: America's Thirty-Year Conflict with Iran*, New York: Penguin Press, 2012, pp. 569-570; Mohammed El-Katiri, *The Future of the Arab Gulf Monarchies in the Age of Uncertainties*, Carlisle, PA; Strategic Studies Institute, U.S. Army War College, June 2013, pp. 28-30.

7. "Putin's Targeted Strike: Russia in the Middle East," *The Economist*, April 18, 2015, p. 41; David E. Sanger, "Role for Russia Gives Iran Talks a Possible Boost," *The New York Times*, November 4, 2014.

8. "Saudi Arabia seeks strategic Chinese Partnership," *Arab News*, Saudi Arabia, March 15, 2014.

9. China has sought limited military-to-military cooperation with Iran, but this is still done at a low-key level. See "China seeks closer military ties with Iran," *Gulf Today*, Sharjah, United Arab Emirates (UAE), October 24, 2014.

10. Sanjeev Miglani, "India clears $8 billion warships project to counter Chinese navy," Reuters, February 18, 2015.

11. "China Sends new anti-piracy mission to Gulf of Aden," *Daily Star*, Beirut, Lebanon, April 3, 2015; Juliet Eilperin, "U.S., Philippines to sign 10-year defense agreement amid rising tensions," *The Washington Post*, April 27, 2014.

12. Kenneth M. Pollack, *Unthinkable: Iran, the Bomb and American Strategy*, New York: Simon & Schuster, 2013, p. 272.

13. "Iraq war 'will be short'," BBC News: *World Edition*, November 15, 2002.

14. Stephen Peter Rosen, "The National Security Generation Gap: Young Americans have become skeptical about the use of U.S. power abroad," *The Wall Street Journal*, March 30, 2014.

15. Greg Jaffe, "In one of final addresses to Army, Gates Describes vision for military's future," *The Washington Post*, February 25, 2011.

16. David Sanger, *Confront and Conceal: Obama's Secret Wars and the Surprising Use of American Power*, New York: Crown Publishers, 2012, p. 421.

17. "FULL TRANSCRIPT: Obama's 2014 State of the Union Address," *The Washington Post*, January 28, 2014.

18. Chris Lawrence, Jill Dougherty, and Tom Cohen, "Hagel: 'We're ready to go' if ordered on Syria Chemical Weapons," *CNN.com*, August 28, 2013; Megan Thee-Brenan, "Poll Shows Isolationist Streak in Americans," *The New York Times*, May 1, 2013.

19. "Growing Support for Campaign Against ISIS—and Possible Use of U.S. Ground Troops," Pew Research Center, February 24, 2015, available from *www.people-press.org*; Eric Planin, "Most Americans Want Obama to Send Ground Troops to Battle ISIS," *Fiscal Times*, March 4, 2015.

20. Anthony H. Cordesman, *Securing the Gulf: Key Threats and Options for Enhanced Cooperation*, Washington DC: Center for Strategic and International Studies, February 19, 2013, pp. iii, 1-3.

21. W. Andrew Terrill, "Iran's Strategy for Saving Asad," *Middle East Journal*, Vol. 69; No. 2, Spring 2015, p. 228.

22. "Lebanon Army vows to fight 'terror' after troops killed," *Arab News*, March 30, 2014.

23. "Saudi Arabia, Egypt deny rift over Assad's rule in Syria," *Khaleej Times*, Dubai, UAE, June 1, 2015.

24. "Kuwait Backs Iraq in fight against ISIL-Min," Kuwait News Agency, June 3, 2015.

25. Steven Erlanger, "Saudi Prince Criticizes Obama Administration, Citing Indecision in Mideast," *The New York Times*, December 15, 2013.

26. "U.S. opposes supply of shoulder-fired missiles to Syrian rebels," *Daily Star*, February 18, 2014; "Saudi-Qatari rivalry, depot raid blamed for FSA reshuffle," *Daily Star*, February 18, 2014.

27. Anne Barnard and Hwaida Saad, "Islamists Seize Control of Syrian City in Northwest," *The New York Times*, April 25, 2015.

28. Carol J. Williams, "US-Saudi Rift papered over by Kerry Visit," *Los Angeles Times*, November 4, 2014.

29. Aaron Blake, "Kerry: Military Action in Syria would be 'unbelievably small'," *The Washington Post*, September 9, 2013.

30. Michael B. Oren, *Ally: My Journey Across the American-Israeli Divide*, New York: Random House, 2015, pp. 344-345.

31. Awad Mustafa, "Saudi Arabia's Aid to Lebanon Presents Challenge for Iran," *Defense News*, January 6, 2014.

32. Nicholas Blanford, "Saudi Arabia promises record $3 billion in military aid to Lebanon," *The Christian Science Monitor*, December 30, 2013.

33. "Arms shipments to begin in April: France," *Daily Star*, February 26, 2015.

34. Hussein Dakroub, "French arms boost anti-terror fight," *Daily Star*, April 20, 2015; Mazin Sidahmed, "French weapons receive red carpet treatment at airport," *Daily Star*, April 21, 2015.

35. "Feeling US Snub, Saudis Strengthen Ties Elsewhere," *Jordan Times*, December 29, 2013.

36. Pollack, p. 150.

37. See remarks by Qatar's emir in "Fight against IS 'will fail if Assad stays,'" *Arab News*, September 27, 2014.

38. Awad Mustafa, "UAE Stiffens Counterterrorism Laws," *Defense News*, July 28, 2014; Associated Press, "Saudi Arabia: Decrees Lay Out Penalties for Fighting Abroad," *The New York Times*, February 4, 2014.

39. "UAE, concerned about militant Islam, passes law against race, faith hate," *Daily Star*, July 7, 2015.

40. Greg Miller, "Fighters are still flocking to Syria," *The Washington Post*, October 31, 2014.

41. Loveday Morris and Rebecca Collard, "U.S. Airstrikes run risk of Helping Syria's Assad," *The Washington Post*, September 24, 2014.

42. Rajiv Chandrasekaran, "Syrian Fighters to fill only a defensive role," *The Washington Post*, October 23, 2014.

43. Thomas Gibbons-Neff, "First Syrians trained by U.S. return to country," *The Washington Post*, July 16, 2015; W. J.

Hennigan and Patrick J. McDonnell, "$500-million program to train anti-Islamic State fighters appears stalled," *The Los Angeles Times*, May 4, 2015.

44. "Fight against IS 'will fail if Assad stays'," *Arab News*, September 27, 2014. "Miteb: Remove Syrian regime to eradicate IS," *Arab News*, November 29, 2014.

45. "US security adviser: US committed to political transition in Syria," *Daily Star*, March 24, 2015.

46. Taylor Luck, "Syria Crisis: Spooked by rebel gains, Jordan doubles down on Islamic State," *The Christian Science Monitor*, May 4, 2015.

47. Phillip Smith, "From Karbala to Sayyida Zaynab: Iraqi Fighters in Syria's Shi'a Militias," *West Point Counterterrorism Center Sentinel*, August 27, 2013, p. 8.

48. Phil Sands, Justin Vela, and Taimur Khan, "Saudi Prince Bandar promised a victory he could not deliver," *The National* (UAE), April 16, 2014.

49. "KSA 'Does Not Fund or Support IS Murderers'," *Arab News*, August 30, 2014.

50. Liz Sly, "Assad's hold on power looks shakier than ever as rebels advance in Syria," *The Washington Post*, April 26, 2015.

51. "Saudi Arabia Warns of Civil War in Iraq," *Khaleej Times*, June 18, 2014.

52. Agency France-Presse (AFP), "Renewed violence as Iraq executes 12 'terrorists'," *Jordan Times*, November 18, 2013; "Anbar Conflict May Spread, warns Iraqi VP al-Hashemi," *Arab News*, January 30, 2014; W. G. Dunlop, "Engulfed in Uncertainty," *Gulf Today*, December 18, 2013.

53. *Make or Break: Iraq's Sunnis and the State*, Brussels, Belgium: International Crisis Group (ICG), August 14, 2013, pp. 15-23.

54. "Saudi slams 'irresponsible' terror accusations by Iraq PM," *Daily Star*, March 10, 2014.

55. Michael Knights, "The ISIL's Stand in the Ramdi-Fallujah Corridor," *West Point Counter Terrorism Center Sentinel*, May 2014, Vol. 7, Issue 5, p. 8.

56. Farnaz Fassihi, A. Ali Tamer, and El-Ghobashy, "Iraq Scrambles to Defend Baghdad—Iraq Says Forces Join Battle Against Advancing Sunni Insurgents Threatening Capital, Holy cities," *The Wall Street Journal*, June 13, 2014.

57. Anthony H. Cordesman, "Key Factors Shaping the President's Islamic State Speech," *Burke Chair Paper*, September 9, 2014, pp. 1-3.

58. Thomas Erdbrink, "As Sunni Militants Threaten its allies in Baghdad, Iran weighs options," *The New York Times*, June 13, 2014.

59. AFP, "Jihadists fighting in Syria, Iraq declare 'caliphate'," *Jordan Times*, June 29, 2014.

60. Ann Barnard and David D. Kirkpatrick, "Arabs give Tepid Support to U.S. fight against ISIS," *The New York Times*, September 12, 2014, p. A-1.

61. Anne Barnard, "Iraqi Drive Against ISIS Reveals Tensions with U.S.," *The New York Times*, March 4, 2015.

62. "Saudi FM urges coalition to face ISIS challenge on the ground," *Daily Star*, March 5, 2015.

63. "Iraq to stay out of Iran-Saudi Conflicts: PM," *The Peninsula*, June 1, 2015.

64. Norman Cigar, *Iraq's Shia Warlords and Their Militias: Political and Security Challenges and Options*, Carlisle, PA., Strategic Studies Institute, U.S. Army War College, 2015, pp. 18-22.

65. Tim Arango, "A Proposal to arm Sunnis fuels talk of an American plot to divide Iraq," *The New York Times*, May 1, 2015.

66. Qassim Abdul-Zahra, "Iraqi leader calls for help against IS," Associated Press, April 14, 2015.

67. "KSA appoints ambassador to Baghdad after 25 years," *Arab News*, April 15, 2015.

68. "Egypt's Sisi says independence for Iraq's Kurds would be 'catastrophic'," *Jordan Times*, July 6, 2014.

69. "Drawing in the neighbors: Syria's conflict," *Economist*, July 4, 2015, p. 39.

70. "109 Saudis among 135 held for abetting terror," *Arab News*, December 8, 2014.

71. Ben Hubbard, "Middle East; Saudi Arabia: ISIS is linked to killings," *The New York Times,* April 25, 2015.

72. "Saudi foils ISIS attack on US embassy, arrests 93," *Daily Star*, April 28, 2015.

73. Angus McDowall, "Riyadh fears ISIS wants sectarian war in kingdom," *Daily Star*, November 19, 2014.

74. Ben Hubbard, "Bomber is Identified in Attack in Kuwait," *The New York Times*, June 29, 2015.

75. "ISIS claims Saudi Arabia mosque bombing," *Daily Star*, May 29, 2015.

76. *Ibid.*

77. "ISIS affiliate hits Shiite mosque in Kuwait, killing 27 people," *Daily Star*, June 27, 2015.

78. "Kuwait seeks death for 11 mosque bombing suspects," Reuters, July 15, 2015.

79. Angus McDowall, "Uncurbed sectarianism prompted village attack say Saudi Shiites," *Daily Star*, November 6, 2014.

80. "Young Saudis warned: Beware of False Jihadis," *Arab News*, February 5, 2014.

81. Ben Hubbard, "Border Clash with Iraqis Kill Seven, Saudis Say," *The New York Times*, January 6, 2015.

82. "Saudi Arabia: al-Qaeda gunman involved in Iraq border attack," *Daily Star*, January 12, 2015.

83. "Saudi Arabia to reopen embassy in Baghdad," *Arab News*, September 14, 2014.

84. "IS poses no threat to Kuwait: Interior Ministry," *Kuwait Times*, January 14, 2015.

85. "Mosque suicide bomber was Saudi, says Riyadh," *Gulf Today*, August 9, 2015.

86. Trita Parsi, *A Single Roll of the Dice: Obama's Diplomacy with Iran*, New Haven, CT, and London, UK: Yale University Press, 2012, pp. 16, 172, 211.

87. Loveday Morris, "Iraq hopes U.S.-Iran nuclear accord will put an end to its divided loyalties," *The Washington Post*, July 15, 2015.

88. "Iran's Nuclear Deal will give Oman a lift," *Times of Oman*, July 14, 2015.

89. Loveday Morris and Hugh Naylor, "Arab States fear 'dangerous' Iranian nuclear deal will shake up the region," *The Washington Post*, July 14, 2015.

90. Robert M. Gates, *Duty: Memoirs of a Secretary at War*, New York: Alfred A. Knopf, 2014, p. 185.

91. *Ibid.*, p. 185.

92. *Ibid.*

93. The GCC includes Bahrain, Kuwait, Oman, Qatar, Saudi Arabia, and the UAE.

94. Ali Noorani, "Saudi joins Israel as target of Jerusalem Day protests," AFP, July 10, 2015.

95. "Iran willing to talk to UAE on Islands Row," *The Peninsula*, May 8, 2013; "UAE denounces Iran lawmakers' visit to islands," *Khaleej Times*, May 7, 2013.

96. Thomas Erdbrink, "Iran Takes Charm Offensive to the Persian Gulf," *The New York Times*, December 4, 2013.

97. "Arab League stresses UAE sovereignty over Iranian-occupied islands," *Khaleej Times*, March 11, 2014; and "Arab Summit backing bolsters UAE aspirations," *Gulf Today*, March 27, 2014.

98. Pollack, p. 88.

99. Cordesman, *Securing the Gulf*, p. 15.

100. "UN Arms Embargo on Iran," Stockholm, Sweden: Stockholm International Peace Research Institute, available from *www. SIPRI.org*, October 11, 2012, accessed August 15, 2013.

101. Barbara Opall-Rome, Aaron Mehta, and Awad Mustafa, "Gulf Nations Eye Iran Acquisition of S-300," *Defense News*, June 1, 2015, p. 6.

102. Anthony H. Cordesman and Martin Kleiber, *Iran's Military Forces and Warfighting Capabilities: The Threat to the Northern Gulf*, Westport, CT: Praeger, 2007, pp. 78-81.

103. "U.S. Blames Iran for new bombs in Iraq," *USA Today*, January 31, 2007; "IED attacks up in Afghanistan, down in Iraq," *Army Times*, November 15, 2007.

104. Marlin Dick, "Iran general killed in failed Deraa attack," *Daily Star*, April 22, 2015; W. Andrew Terrill, "Iran's Strategy for Saving Asad," *Middle East Journal*, Vol. 69, No. 2, Spring 2015, pp. 230-231.

105. Cigar, pp. 23-26.

106. Michael R. Gordon, "U.S. Plans Military Drills in Eastern Europe," *The New York Times*, April 19, 2014.

107. "Kerry promises Arab allies: No grand bargain with Iran," *Daily Star*, March 6, 2015.

108. AFP, "Britain to Reopen Embassy in Tehran," *Jordan Times*, June 17, 2014.

109. Thomas Erdbrink, "Iran Takes Charm Offensive to the Persian Gulf," *The New York Times*, December 4, 2013.

110. Al Jazeera, "Gulf States Hesitant about Iranian Overtures," *Gulf Research Center Newsletter*, December 9, 2013.

111. *Ibid.*

112. Ben Hubbard, "Arab World Split over Iran Nuclear Deal," *The New York Times*, July 14, 2015.

113. Mark Landler, "On Iran and Syria, Tests of Diplomacy Intertwine," *The New York Times*, December 19, 2013.

114. Thomas Erdbrink, "Iran Agrees to Provide Data on Its Detonators," *The New York Times*, February 10, 2014.

115. Bozorgmehr Sharafedin Nouri, "US Disturbed by Iranian leader's criticism after deal," Reuters, July 21, 2015.

116. "Iran's role in Iraq could be positive: US general," *Daily Star*, March 4, 2015.

117. "US sends aircraft carrier to help Iraq," *The Peninsula*, June 15, 2014.

118. Loveday Morris, "Iraq sees good reason to embrace nuclear agreement," *The Washington Post*, July 16, 2015.

119. "Prince Turki: Gulf states 'must balance threat from Iran'," *Arab News*, April 24, 2014.

120. Fareed Zakaria, "Saudi Arabia's Bluff," *The Washington Post*, June 14, 2015.

121. Tim Craig, "Defying Saudis, Pakistani lawmakers vote to stay out of Yemen," *The Washington Post*, April 10, 2015.

122. "Survey: Saudis consider Iran their top enemy, not Israel," *Daily Star*, June 4, 2015.

123. "The New Frenemies; Israel and Saudi Arabia," *Economist*, July 13, 2015, p. 47.

124. Karin Laub, "Israel, Jordan discreetly foster ties amid regional chaos," *Daily Star*, June 23, 2015.

125. Michael Morell, *The Great War of Our Time: The CIA's Fight against Terrorism from al Qa'ida to ISIS*, New York: Twelve, 2015, p. 185.

126. David E. Sanger, *Confront and Conceal: Obama's Secret Wars and Surprising Use of American Power*, New York: Crown Publishers, 2012, pp. 302-303.

127. *Ibid.*, p. 302.

128. William C. Taylor, *Military Responses to the Arab Uprisings and the Future of Civil Military Relations in the Middle East*, New York: Palgrave Macmillan, 2014, p. 125.

129. Carrie Rosefsky Wickham, *The Muslim Brotherhood: Evolution of an Islamist Movement*, Princeton, NJ, and Oxford, UK: Princeton University Press, p. 264.

130. Gregory Aftandilian, *Egypt's New Regime and the Future of the U.S.-Egyptian Strategic Relationship*, Carlisle, PA: Strategic Studies Institute, U.S. Army War College, 2013, p. 11.

131. Wickham, p. 264.

132. An Egyptian criminal court convicted Morsi of a number of crimes, including inciting violence, but acquitted him of premeditated murder. He must still stand trial on additional

charges. He has been sentenced to 20 years in prison but could receive additional sentences. David D. Kirkpatrick and Thomas Merna, "Egyptian leader deposed by Army in '13 gets 20 year prison term," *The New York Times*, April 22, 2015.

133. David D. Kirkpatrick and Thomas Merna, "Egyptian leader deposed by army in '13 gets a 20-year prison term," *The New York Times*, April 22, 2015.

134. David D. Kirkpatrick, "Egyptian Court Confirms Death Penalty for Morsi," *The New York Times*, June 17, 2015.

135. See comments on Egypt by Secretary of State Kerry to various Arab leaders in "Jordan, US call for cooperation to restore security in Iraq," *Jordan Times*, June 22, 2014.

136. Michael Georgy and Tom Perry, "Egypt's Sisi says Muslim Brotherhood is finished," Reuters, May 6, 2014; Hamza Hendawi, "Egypt's el-Sisi: No Reconciliation with Islamists," *Daily Star*, June 8, 2014.

137. "Leading anti-Mubarak activist sentenced to 15 years in jail," *Jordan Times*, June 11, 2014.

138. "Gulf states give Egypt $6B in aid," *Daily Star*, April 24, 2015; "King Abdullah calls El-Sisi to pledge economic support," *Arab News*, June 7, 2014.

139. David D. Kirkpatrick, "529 Egyptians Sentenced to Death in One killing," *The New York Times*, March 25, 2004; AFP, "Egypt Court condemns 188 to death," *Jordan Times*, December 2, 2014; "Egypt: Of Judges and generals," *Economist*, March 29, 2014, p. 48.

140. Elliott Abrams, "A Pinochet in Egypt?" *The Washington Post*, April 26, 2015.

141. Associated Press, "Egypt moves to restrict Ramadan sermons," *Jordan Times*, June 29, 2014.

142. Ernesto Londono, "U.S. to partially resume military aid to Egypt," *The Washington Post*, April 22, 2014.

143. "Egypt president welcomes return of US military aid," *Daily Star*, April 1, 2015.

144. Editorial Board, "Mixed Messages in Egypt's Military Aid," *The New York Times*, April 1, 2015.

145. Gregory Aftandilian, *Assessing Egyptian Public Support for Security Crackdown in the Sinai*, Carlisle, PA: Strategic Studies Institute, U.S. Army War College, 2008, p. 8.

146. *Ibid.*, pp. 11-15.

147. Eric Schmitt, David D. Kirkpatrick, "Islamic State Sprouting Limbs Beyond its Base," *The New York Times*, February 15, 2015.

148. AFP, "Israel raises alarm over Sinai-Gaza cooperation," *Jordan Times*, January 16, 2012.

149. Unproven rumors also exist that Morsi had established a truce with Ansar Beit al-Maqdis. See Aftandilian, *Assessing Egyptian Public Support for Security Crackdown in the Sinai*, pp. 9-10.

150. Yusri Mohamed, "Attacks in Egypt's Sinai kill 33 security personnel," Reuters, October 24, 2014.

151. Kareem Fahim, "Protest is Muted as Egypt Levels Border Area in Sinai," *The New York Times*, October 31, 2014.

152. Ashraf Swellam and Brian Rohan, "Massive assault on Egypt army in Sinai kills 64 troops," *The Washington Post*, July 1, 2015.

153. Kristen Chick, "Ahmadinejad visits Cairo: How Sect tempers Islamist ties between Egypt, Iran," *The Christian Science Monitor*, February 5, 2013,

154. David D. Kirkpatrick, "Egypt Launches Strike in Libya on ISIS Branch," *The New York Times*, February 17, 2015.

155. *Ibid.*

156. David D. Kirkpatrick, "Islamic State Video Appears to Show Execution of Christians in Libya," *The New York Times*, April 20, 2015.

157. Hassan Morajea; Erin Cunningham, "Militants fill void in Libya's Civil War," *The Washington Post*, June 7, 2015.

158. *Libya: Getting Geneva Right*, Brussels, Belgium: ICG, February 2015, p. 9.

159. David D. Kirkpatrick and Suliman Ali Zway, "Western Officials Alarmed by ISIS' Advances in Libya," *The New York Times*, June 1, 2015.

160. Ulf Laessing and Ayman al-Warfalli, "Expulsion from Derna May Show limits for ISIS in Libya," *Daily Star*, July 25, 2015; "Libya Officials: Jihadis Driving IS from Eastern Stronghold," *The New York Times*, July 30, 2015.

161. Dion Nissenbaum and Maria Abi-Habib, "Islamic State Sends Fighters to Libya," *The Wall Street Journal*, May 19, 2015.

162. "65 percent of Yemeni Voters Picks a New President," *Khaleej Times*, February 25, 2012.

163. W. Andrew Terrill, "Drones Over Yemen: Military Benefits and Political Costs," *Parameters: US Army War College Quarterly*, Winter/Spring 2013, pp. 17-23.

164. "Yemen President Vows to Pursue al-Qaeda-linked Militants," *Jordan Times*, March 6, 2012.

165. Ellen Knickmeyer and Hakim Almasmari, "Attack on Military is a Blow to Yemen," *The Wall Street Journal*, May 22, 2012.

166. "Al Qaeda in Yemen on the Run as Military regains control Over 2 of its Strongholds," *The Washington Post*, June 12, 2012; Also see "Yemen Tribes Denounce Threats to Saudi Security," *Saudi Gazette*, January 6, 2010;

167. Barak A. Salmoni, Bryce Loidolt, and Madeleine Wells, *Regime and Periphery in Northern Yemen: The Huthi Phenomenon*, Santa Monica, CA: RAND Corporation, 2010, pp. 89-96.

168. *Ibid.*, especially Chap. 5.

169. Robert F. Worth, "Yemen Seems to Reject Cease-Fire with Rebels," *The New York Times*, February 1, 2010.

170. W. Andrew Terrill, "Iranian Involvement in Yemen," *Orbis*, Summer 2014, pp. 429-438.

171. Michael R. Gordon and Eric Schmitt, "Tensions Flare Between Allies in U.S. Coalition," *The New York Times*, April 16, 2015.

172. Associated Press, "Thousands rally in Yemen over ended fuel subsidies," *The Washington Post*, August 18, 2014.

173. Roger Owen, *The Rise and Fall of Arab Presidents for Life*, Cambridge, MA: Harvard University Press, 2012, pp. 107-108.

174. Ali Aboluhom, "Supporters of Ahmed Saleh call on him to run for President," *Yemen Times*, March 11, 2015; Associated Press, "Yemen protesters demand return of former autocrat's son," *The Washington Post*, March 10, 2015.

175. AFP, "Shiite rebel seizure of Yemen a 'gift' for Tehran?" *Jordan Times*, September 25, 2014.

176. Ali Ibrahim Al-Moshki, "UAE revokes Ahmed Ali Saleh's Diplomatic Immunity," *Yemen Times*, April 8, 2015.

177. "US says no plans to move embassy in Yemen to Aden," *Daily Star*, March 3, 2015.

178. "Iran's nuclear deal puts Saudis on edge," Reuters, July 15, 2015.

179. Faisal J. Abbas, "Why Operation Decisive Storm was needed in Yemen," *Saudi Gazette*, March 27, 2015.

180. Katharine Houreld, "Iran minister meets Pakistan military chief amid Yemen dilemma," *Daily Star*, April 9, 2015; Tim Craig, "Pakistani lawmakers choose to remain neutral in Yemen," *The Washington Post*, April 11, 2015.

181. David D. Kirkpatrick, "Egypt says it is ready to send air, sea and ground forces to Yemen," *The New York Times*, March 27, 2015.

182. Awad Mustafa, "Evidence of Saudi-led Forces in Yemen grows," *Defense News*, July 27-August 3, 2015.

183. Saeed al-Batati and Kareem Fahim, "Foreign Ground Troops Join Yemen Fight," *The New York Times*, August 4, 2015; "Three Emiratis martyred in Yemen," *Khaleej Times*, August 9, 2015.

184. "U.S. Expands intelligence sharing with Saudis in Yemen operation," Reuters, April 11, 2015.

185. "US Steps up arms shipments to support Decisive Storm," *Arab News*, April 8, 2015.

186. "US to Tehran: Hands off Yemen," *Arab News*, April 10, 2015.

187. "Kerry allays Gulf concerns," *Arab News*, April 6, 2015.

188. Hugh Naylor, "Yemen conflict's risk for Saudis: 'Their Vietnam'," *The Washington Post*, April 9, 2015.

189. For an interesting history of the rise of the Southern Independence movement, see *Yemen's Southern Question: Avoiding a Breakdown*, Brussels, Belgium: ICG, 2013.

190. "Yemen at War: Crisis Group Middle Eastern Briefing," Brussels, Belgium: ICG, March 27, 2015, p. 2.

191. "Saudi-led coalition keeps up strikes on Yemen Rebels," *Daily Star*, April 23, 2015.

192. Michael R. Gordon and Thomas Erdbrink, "Yemen Crisis Looms as Kerry Meets with Iranian Counterpart on Nuclear Accord," *The New York Times*, April 28, 2015.

193. David D. Kirkpatrick, "Tensions Between Iran and Saudi Arabia Deepen over Conflict in Yemen," *The New York Times*, April 10, 2015.

194. Ben Hubbard, "King Salman Upends Status Quo in Region and the Royal Family," *The New York Times*, May 11, 2015.

195. Mohammed Ghobari, "Al Qaeda and Houthis clash in central Yemen: Residents," Reuters, October 16, 2014.

196. "An Exceptional franchise; al-Qaeda in the Arabian Peninsula," *Economist*, April 25, 2015, p. 46.

197. "Al Qaeda suspects among 1,200 who escaped from Yemeni Prison," *Arab News*, July 1, 2015.

198. Zaid al-Alayaa and Laura King, "Militants free 300 Yemen inmates; al Qaeda attacks a southeastern prison as Houthi rebels surge into a key port," *The Los Angeles Times*, April 3, 2015.

199. Saeed al-Batati, "Qaeda Affiliate pushes military out of major Yemeni city," *The New York Times*, April 4, 2015.

200. "New 'Green Brigade' of ISIS claims Yemen attack," *Daily Star*, April 23, 2015.

201. "Daesh attacks Houthi mosques," *Arab News*, June 21, 2015.

202. "U.S. departure from Yemen weakens relations, terrorist fight, general says," *The Washington Times*, March 3, 2015.

203. "U.S. envoy to Yemen to work from Jeddah after embassy's closure," Reuters, March 3, 2015.

204. "Arabia Influx: The War in Yemen," *Economist*, April 18, 2015, p. 42; Declan Walsh, "Despite Errors, Drones Decimate Weakened Qaeda," *The New York Times*, April 25, 2015.

205. Greg Miller, "Drone Rules: Is 'near certainty' enough to pull the trigger?" *The Washington Post*, April 24, 2015.

206. Greg Miller, "Al-Qaeda leader was not target of strike," *The Washington Post*, June 18, 2015.

207. Ali al-Mujahed and Hugh Naylor, "In Yemen's grinding war, if the bombs don't get you, the water shortages will," *The Washington Post*, July 23, 2015.

208. "Saleh in talks on Yemen peace," *The Peninsula*, July 24, 2015.

209. "US set to hit Daesh group from ground," *Khaleej Times*, February 16, 2015.

210. "Kuwait: Security and Foreign Forces," *Jane's Sentinel Security Assessment – The Gulf States*, June 6, 2015.

211. "Fund US Deterrent Programs," *Defense News,* June 29, 2015, p. 20.

212. "News Transcript: Remarks by Secretary Hagel at the Manama Dialogue form Manama Bahrain," U.S. Department of Defense, December 7, 2013, available from *www.defense.gov*. For Gulf reaction to Hagel's speech, see "US to maintain 35,000 troops in Gulf," *The Peninsula,* December 8, 2013.

213. Awad Mustafa and Barbara Opall-Rome, "Security Assurances, but no Military Bonanza for Regional Allies," *Defense News*, July 20, 2015, p. 1.

214. *Ibid.*, and Craig Whitlock, "Carter Summons U.S. military commanders, diplomats to Kuwait, *The Washington Post*, February 22, 2015.

215. Mustafa and Opall-Rome, p. 2.

216. Crist, pp. 569-570.

217. "US-led Gulf Naval Exercises Underway," Associated Press, May 6, 2013.

218. Michael R. Gordon and David D. Kirpatrick, "Kerry Warns Egypt Human Rights Abuses Can Hurt Fight Against Terrorism," *The New York Times*, August 3, 2015.

219. When the author visited Iraq in 2008, he was amused by Iraqi officers who continually addressed U.S. Navy captains serving as staff officers as "colonel" despite ongoing efforts to correct them.

220. Michael R. Gordon and Thom Shanker, "U.S. to Keep Warplanes in Jordan, Pressing Syria," *The New York Times*, June 16, 2013.

221. Donna Miles, "Advance Headquarters Elements Operating in Jordan," U.S. Department of Defense Press Release, April 18, 2013, available from *www.defense.gov*, accessed June 10, 2013.

222. Cordesman, *Securing the Gulf*, p. 2.

223. General Raymond Odierno, "Regionally Aligned Forces: A New Model for Building Partnerships," *Army Live, The Official Blog of the U.S. Army*, March 22, 2012, accessed March 14, 2015.

224. Colonel Phillip A. Chambers and Colonel Tarn D. Warren "RAF Movement and Maneuver Warfighting Function" in Dr. Larry Miller, Gregory L. Cantwell, Colonel Tarn D. Warren, and Colonel Mark E. Orwat, eds., *Regionally Aligned Forces: Concept Viability and Implementation*, Carlisle, PA: Carlisle Compendia of Collaborative Research, 2015, p. 35.

225. Lieutenant Colonel Mark B. Parker and John A. Bonin, "RAF and Mission Command," in Miller *et al.*, *Regionally Aligned Forces*, p. 26.

226. Colonel Gregory M. Smith and Colonel Tarn D. Warren, "RAF and Fires Warfighting Function" in Miller *et al.*, *Regionally Aligned Forces*, p. 59.

227. Emma Sky, *The Unraveling: High Hopes and Missed Opportunities in Iraq*, New York: PublicAffairs, 2015, p. 136.

228. Colonel James B. Botters and Colonel Mark A. Haseman, "RAF and Intelligence Warfighting Functions," in Miller *et al.*, *Regionally Aligned Forces*, p. 48.

229. Smith and Warren in Miller *et al.*, *Regionally Aligned Forces*, p. 58.

230. Sky, p. 44.

231. *Ibid.*

232. Brigadier General Wayne W. Grigsby, Jr., Colonel Patrick Matlock, Lieutenant Colonel Christopher Norrie, and Major Karen Radka, "Mission Command in the Regionally Aligned Division Headquarters," *Military Review*, November-December 2013, pp. 3-9.

233. C. Todd Lopez, "1st Armored Division Troops aligned with CENTCOM ready for Eager Lion Kick-Off," official home page of the U.S. Army, available from *www.army.mil*, June 3, 2013, accessed July 29, 2014.

234. See "King Abdullah II Special Operations Training Center," available from *www.kasotc.com*, accessed August 2, 2014.

235. Casey L. Coombs, "Yemen to Get UAVs from the U.S.," *Aerospace Daily & Defense Report*, September 26, 2012; Anthony H. Cordesman, Robert M. Shelala II, and Omar Mohamed, *U.S. and Iranian Strategic Competition: Yemen and U.S. Security*, Washington DC: Center for Strategic and International Studies, August 8, 2013, pp. 10-15.

236. Loveday Morris, "Investigation finds 50,000 'ghost' soldiers in Iraqi army, prime minister says," *The Washington Post*, November 30, 2014.

237. John McLaughlin, "How the Islamic State Could Win," *The Washington Post*, May 28, 2015.

238. For an excellent discussion of how U.S. troops became increasingly effective at counterinsurgency operations over time in Iraq, see James A. Russell, *Innovation, Transformation and War: Counterinsurgency Operations in Anbar and Ninewa Provinces, Iraq, 2005-2007*, Stanford, CA: Stanford Security Studies, 2011.

239. The GCC has taken the lead in providing support and financial help for Yemen's transition to a more stable government including brokering the departure from power of longtime strongman, President Ali Abdullah Saleh.

240. "Yemen Army Retakes al Qaeda Bastions," *Jordan Times,* June 12, 2012.

241. The author has been consistently impressed by the seriousness, commitment, and integrity of Yemeni officers he has met at the U.S. Army War College and elsewhere.

242. Associated Press, "Iraqi Official: Baghdad would welcome U.S. military help as Pentagon Considers sending trainers," *The Washington Post,* June 27, 2013.

243. Russell, p. 101.

244. *Ibid.,* p. 174.

245. *Ibid.,* p. 122.

246. Rick Gladstone, "Iraqi Envoy Calls on U.S. to Strengthen Relationship," *The New York Times,* April 4, 2014.

247. Paul McLeay, "US, Iranian Drones Crowd Iraqi Air Space," *Defense News,* July 28, 2014, p. 1.

248. "UAE to set up rehab centres for those 'lured' by terror cells," *Khaleej Times,* August 25, 2014.

249. Agencies, "Jordan, US to cooperate in upgrading border defence capabilities," *Jordan Times,* May 14, 2014.

250. "US concerned about Iran missiles, committed to Gulf security," *Jordan Times,* April 27, 2014.

251. "US offers help for Gulf-wide missile defense capability," *Arab News,* April 28, 2014.

252. "US approves arms sales to Saudi Arabia," *Daily Star,* July 31, 2015.

253. Dania Saadi, "Lockheed Martin set to deliver missile defence system to UAE," *The National* (UAE), December 7, 2014.

254. Jeremy Binnie, "Idex 2015: Saudi, Qatari THAAD contracts in the pipeline," *Jane's 360,* February 24, 2015.

255. Thomas L. McNaugher, "Ballistic Missiles and Chemical Weapons: The Legacy of the Iran-Iraq War," *International Security*, Fall 1990, pp. 5-34; W. Andrew Terrill, "The Gulf War and Ballistic Missile Proliferation," *Comparative Strategy*, April-June 1992, pp. 163-176.

256. Max Fisher, "What Syria's Scud Missile launches tell us about the regime's thinking," *The Washington Post*, December 12, 2012; Ben Hubbard and Hwaida Saad, "Syrian Government Blamed for Ballistic Missile Attack," *The New York Times*, July 28, 2013.

257. Kenneth Katzman, *The United Arab Emirates (UAE) Issues for U.S. Policy*, Washington, DC: Congressional Research Service, March 18, 2013, pp. 11-12; Suzanne Maloney, "Thinking the Unthinkable: The Gulf States and the Prospect of a Nuclear Iran," *Middle East Memo of the Saban Center at Brookings,* Brookings Institution, January 27, 2013, p. 11.

258. Andrea Shalal and Matt Spetalnick, "Obama expected to push for Gulf missile defense at U.S. summit," *Daily Star*, May 6, 2015.

259. As cited in Andrea Shalal, "Missile Shield for Gulf to take years, and heavy U.S. commitment," Reuters, May 16, 2015.

U.S. ARMY WAR COLLEGE

Major General William E. Rapp
Commandant

*****

STRATEGIC STUDIES INSTITUTE
and
U.S. ARMY WAR COLLEGE PRESS

Director
Professor Douglas C. Lovelace, Jr.

Director of Research
Dr. Steven K. Metz

Author
Dr. W. Andrew Terrill

Editor for Production
Dr. James G. Pierce

Publications Assistant
Ms. Rita A. Rummel

*****

Composition
Mrs. Jennifer E. Nevil